A SOULWORKER'S COMPANION

A Soulworker's Companion

A YEAR OF SPIRITUAL DISCOVERY

BettyClare Moffatt

WILDCAT CANYON PRESS
Berkeley, California
A Division of Circulus Publishing Group, Inc.

LIBRARY OF CONGRESS CATALOGING-IN-PUBLICATION DATA
Moffatt, BettyClare.
    A soulworker's companion: a year of spiritual discovery /
    BettyClare Moffatt.
        p.   cm.
    Includes bibliographical references.
    ISBN I-885171-11-0
    I. Spiritual life.   2. Moffatt, BettyClare.   I. Title.
BL624.M635 1996   96-3275
291-4'4—dc20   CIP

Distributed to the trade by Publishers Group West
10 9 8 7 6 5 4 3 2 I
Printed in the United States of America

PUBLISHER: Julienne Bennett
SENIOR EDITOR: Roy M. Carlisle
COPYEDITOR: Jean M. Blomquist
COVER DESIGN: John Miller, Big Fish
COVER PHOTOGRAPH © Junshi Nakamichi/Photonica,
used by permission.
INTERIOR DESIGN: Gordon Chun Design

CONTENTS

To my beloved mother,

HELEN EDWINA THOMAS COOK,

in enduring love.

ACKNOWLEDGMENTS

I would like to express my heartfelt gratitude to all the people at Circulus Publishing Group, Inc. who helped in the creation of *A Soulworker's Companion,* and recognized this book as the next step after *Soulwork.*

For Julie, Roy, Tamara, Holly, Jean, Gordon, Suzanne, John and all who share the vision of creating beautiful books to serve the world, many thanks!

Thousands of books line my walls, spilling a wealth of ideas, inspiration and information. Favorite sources of quotations for this book include *Sunbeams: A Book of Quotations,* edited by Sy Safransky (Berkeley, CA: North Atlantic Books, 1990); *Living Quotations for Christians,* edited by Sherwood Eliot Wirt and Kersten Beckstrom (New York: Harper & Row, 1974); and my yearly, much-used editions of the *Master Mind Goal Achiever's Journal* (Warren, MI: Master Mind Publishing Co.). Any quotations found in this book that could not be traced back to primary sources are gratefully acknowledged from the books cited above.

INTRODUCTION

In late 1993 and early 1994 I wrote a series of personal essays called *Soulwork*. They came to me on long, meditative walks. They came out of the depths of my heart and soul as I struggled and questioned and affirmed my way back to stability, balance, and joy after a ten-year series of challenges. These essays were like a gift from Spirit. They came to me out of the clear blue sky. They taught me what I already knew but had forgotten about my connection with the Source of my being. Sad, funny, ironic, passionate, despairing, wondering, questioning, resolving, life-affirming; they were my Soulwork. They were my connection with Spirit. They were a way for me to put the fruit of many years of spiritual questioning into form. I felt then as I do now, that Soulwork is life work.

Soulwork was published immediately after a series of synchronistic events. Soon, many readers wrote to me personally and told me their stories as well. "Yes!" they said. "Yes! This is the way it is. Thank you, dear friend. But what do I do now?"

A Soulworker's Companion is my response to these letters and to discussions during my readings. It is the next step after *Soulwork*. I began to think that in my own personal prayer practice, I could use a map, a blueprint if you will, that would help me to focus on the soul qualities, the soul attributes, that I wanted to continue developing. Being practical as well as mystical, I came up with fifty areas which I wanted to continue exploring in my walks, my meditations, my contemplative times, and in my action-filled times as well. It seemed to me that there were universal themes of soul progress that had very little to do with specific religious affiliation, age, race, or gender. Because I am a woman and write personally about my life concerns, this book will, I hope, appeal to women everywhere. Because the quotations and prayers I found along the way were written mostly by men, their wisdom and point of view are also represented.

The qualities of the soul are alive and dynamic, not passive, dreary, dead. These are no Sunday School lessons. This is powerful work: growing a soul, designing a life, composing a path to God. When I close my eyes and think of what the fifty qualities of the soul look like in the everyday lives of readers, this is what I see:

A woman creating a tapestry of intricate scenes, weaving her self into every jeweled design.

A man watering and weeding a garden, growing his soul with every motion of stooping and standing.

A child opening a series of boxes, each one a surprise, gaily wrapped, containing world upon world of delight and challenge.

A group of women making a quilt, piecing and stitching remnants of country wisdom and generations of family and friends into a time-honored, homespun pattern.

A mapmaker, charting his way into an unknown sea.

An elderly woman, dreaming over a jigsaw puzzle, carefully fitting each piece into a pattern that tells her life.

An architect, drafting a plan that will create a cathedral from his meticulous drawings.

A series of banners unfurling, flags of every shape, size, and color, fifty in all, carried and held aloft joyfully and proudly by diverse and dynamic souls.

A mosaic of colors and words that, when put together, form stained-glass windows that let the light shine through the prism of their patterns and reflect their colors on all who stand near them.

Which is your image? What is your way? Where does your soul long to explore?

May you uncover and discover and recover qualities of your soul that have long waited to be recognized, accepted, developed, practiced, integrated, known, used, loved. I will be using this book with you on our shared journey.

Blessings!
BettyClare Moffatt

This book is meant to be a companion to you along your soul's journey. The heartfelt personal stories are designed to help you access your own inner story, your own connections to Spirit. It is your book. These are your soul qualities. You can approach it in an orderly fashion, working through each week of the year. Or you can dip into this book at random, allowing your inner self to guide you to what you need next in your soul's progress. You can write in it, question it, ruminate in it, memorize its passages. You can use it as a daybook, or start all over with it the following year. This book is a gentle companion, a fellow traveler, a friendly explorer.

To help you access the fifty positive qualities of the soul, the following spiritual tools are suggested. These are prayer, meditation, visualization, guided imagery, affirmation, intention, and contemplation. Each is valuable, each is available to us on our soul journey. You may also utilize your own thoughtful and reflective techniques that have worked for you. I use the tools of listening, observing, and experiencing to help me on my soul journey. I learn from every person I meet, every book I read, every situation I encounter.

A crucial ingredient in our journey is inner exploration. Prayer, meditation, and all points, tools, and processes in-between offer ways to access the mental, emotional, and spiritual aspects of ourselves to help us become whole.

Here is an explanation of basic inner work avenues available to the sincere spiritual seeker.

Prayer

Prayer is the art of talking to God. It can be formal or informal. You can pray in a holy place of worship, you can repeat written words from holy sources. Or you can simply call out "God help me!" Prayer can be a healing, an invocation, a thanksgiving, a song, an intercession. Prayer can be for us, as in a cry of repentance and resolve, we ask "God forgive me!" Prayer can be for others, as when we ask for healing and comfort for loved ones and friends. Prayer can be both blessing and ritual. Prayer is an acknowledgment of God's presence and power in our lives, by whatever name we call our Creator. If we do not feel comfortable reaching out in prayer to God or Jesus Christ, we can call on a Higher Power, Oneness, the Christ Consciousness, the Light, the Holy Spirit, Angels and Archangels or our own personal Guardian Angel.

Meditation

Meditation is the art of listening to God. In meditation, you are not concerned with begging, pleading, or cajoling God to answer your prayers. Instead, meditation is an act of acceptance and receptivity. It is a releasing process, in which we let go of our rational, logical, everyday methods of dealing with the outer world and instead allow a true reality, a new perception, to come into our hearts and minds. While there are various techniques used to reach the meditative process, they are not the end result. They are only tools of access and awareness that can help you to a state of inner calm and inner receptivity, a state of listening and inner peace. As your awareness grows, so will your meditations change and deepen in joy and wisdom, whatever form they take, whether you are counting breaths, watching a flower unfold in your mind, contemplating light, repeating holy sounds, or just sitting in the silence. Meditation is communion. Meditation is accessing the Divine.

Visualization and Guided Imagery

Visualization is the art of creating a picture of your good (whatever that may be at any given moment) in your mind. It is a process of taking thought and imagination, in all its unformed, unfocused elasticity, and creating vivid images in your mind, which you can then use as a blueprint for goal-setting and for making creative changes in your life.

Visualization is more than daydreaming, although every kind of dreaming can help you to stretch your perceptions. Visualization is focused intent. Some spiritual teachers tell us that we are always creating our own versions of reality, in one way or another, usually unconsciously. Visualization often includes speaking and writing out your good, including goal-setting to assist you in changing conditions that no longer serve you, that you may have brought into your life in order to learn lessons at a deep soul level. Visualization, while often used by athletes, sculptors, painters, is not confined to any one profession. We are all creators and visualizers, whether we are children who can see ourselves grown up or a caring teacher who inspires the bright potential within the struggling student.

Guided imagery helps you to set a scene in order to ask your inner self to bring to you whatever you specifically need to solve a problem, and then allow you to dialogue with the person or situation you have brought to mind.

I use visualization by preparing myself each day in my work as writer. I take a few quiet moments to turn within and to see, in my mind's eye, the finished book that I am writing now. I see the right words in the right order, the interviews, the research, the inspiration, the insights. When I write, I write from myself to the reader. My aim in this kind of daily visualization and inspiration is to connect with the reader. I see the reader receiving even as

I am giving. This way of working aligns me with the reader, instead of isolating me in a tangle of words. The ideas flow when I remember that I am giving to others instead of just chasing words around in my own mind.

Affirmation and Intention

Affirmation is asking for your good in the continuing present. It is often used along with visualization and goal-setting. Many prayers and meditations are also affirmations. They are also intentions. Yet intention goes a step beyond affirming, desiring, wishing. Intention is determination. Intention is making a conscious choice for your continuing good. A clear and focused intent is a creative tool for bringing your hopes, dreams, and wishes into manifestation.

Contemplation

Contemplation is taking a thought, a phrase, a sentence, a quotation, a story, and reflecting on its meaning until you have incorporated the meaning into your consciousness. Of course you can also contemplate a sunset, an object, a painting. You can contemplate a problem until you wring the juice out of it and go through the other side to a solution. You can contemplate another person, but it is risky to dwell on another's imperfections or perfections. Contemplation is a way of assimilating the world around you. You can make a choice. You can choose what you put into your mind and heart just as you choose what you put into your mouth. The discerning use of contemplation helps you to become wise.

Everything you imagine is a way of projecting a probable future. That is why it is so important to learn to change the pictures we habitually carry in our minds that do not correspond to the reality we want. This is an ongoing process, and includes identifying habitual thought patterns and reactions that do not serve us, and gradually, patiently, without judgment, beginning to clear out and replace those patterns of negativity and stuckness with more free-flowing harmonious ways of reacting to the world. Practicing prayer, meditation, visualization, guided imagery, affirmation, intention, and contemplation can help to create the conditions in the inner that lead to new conditions in the outer.

One powerful way to look within yourself for the answers to your problems is simply to stop and ask yourself, when faced with any number of decisions during the day, "What is the truth of this situation?" This one simple question, if utilized on a consistent basis, can save countless hours of anguish. When a solution to a situation has eluded me for some time, especially if it has great emotional content for me, I get up very early and walk outside at dawn and ask this question again and again until I arrive at a peaceful answer, an answer that is the highest and the best for all concerned in the situation. So awareness techniques can be both simple and practical.

One more thing. Although inner awareness techniques are immensely valuable to learn and practice during our lives, they are only a part of our journey. For we are not techniques. We are multidimensional, feeling, yearning, acting, and reacting beings. We use what we have in the house of our being, and then we go forward in ever-increasing light and love to right action in the outer world. We learn to balance the inner and the outer. We learn to balance our own needs with the needs of others. As we continue, an alchemy takes place, a true union of the best and the brightest within us combined with the best that we can do and be in the world around us. This is a lifetime journey, this soulworker's journey. It is the only journey there is.

Choosing Soulwork

THERE'S A GREAT DEAL OF TALK about the soul these days—talk about finding your soul, caring for your soul, "growing the soul." All of this talk seems to be about developing, examining, working with your soul. I could list various learned sources which would instruct you how to do what I call "Soulwork," but unless and until you have experienced the work of your own soul, I doubt that they would have much meaning for you.

Soulwork, or growing the soul, seems to be an abstract concept. However, when I first heard the term "growing the soul," my mind involuntarily presented me with a physical image of what that might be, perhaps something detectible on my body. It would weigh me down and set me apart. The idea of growing a soul seemed mystifying to me.

Later I came to see the idea of growing a soul as growing a flower in a garden. Weed around it, water it, let the sun fall upon it, talk to it a little, sprinkle encouragement and feed it, and then a beautiful flower would emerge, to be admired and enjoyed by all. But what if the flower did not grow but died before it bloomed? Or what if the flower was not a flower at all but a poisonous, noxious weed. What then? Ah, metaphor!

I like what John Bradshaw has to say about spirituality, because his words convey the multiplicity of all that we think, feel, say, and do as part of our soul's growth, our spiritual adventure: "What is spirituality? I believe it has to do with our life-style. I believe that life is ever-unfolding and growing. So spirituality is about expansion and growth. It is about love, truth, goodness, beauty, giving and caring. Spirituality is about wholeness and completion. Spirituality is our ultimate human need. It pushes us to transcend ourselves, and to become grounded in the ultimate source of reality. Most call that source God."

I believe that we continually develop, whether as a flower, weed, or any other visual image you wish to invoke. We develop as fourfold people: physically, mentally, emotionally, and spiritually. And the process of spiritual development is the one least likely to be observed, tracked, measured. In fact, I don't think that there are any measurements at all for the soul. I believe, instead, that the nature of the soul is to experience, express, and expand. And through its experiences in form and its expression in the world, the soul is gently and irrevocably led to an expansion of its capabilities, into an expansion of joy and service.

But how? This book offers some tools for the journey—through story and prayer, through intention and affirmation, through the wise words of others who have gone before and left their words to light a path for us. You will find many expressions of the soul's journey throughout this book. Each is a unique viewpoint, an angle of vision, a turning point, a tried and true and tested version of life. Choose which you like. Each road will lead you home.

Am I willing to pledge myself to a year of Soulwork through the contemplation of fifty positive soul qualities?
Am I ready for an unfolding of my spiritual life?

"We have not even to risk the adventure alone, for the heroes of all time have gone before us; the labyrinth is thoroughly known: we have only to follow the thread of the hero path. And where we had thought to find an abomination, we shall find a god: where we had thought to slay another, we shall slay ourselves; where we had thought to travel outward, we shall come to the center of our own existence; and where we had thought to be alone, we shall be with all the world."

–JOSEPH CAMPBELL

"Think of what you are doing as entering into partnership with Divine Intelligence, a partnership in which you begin to share your concerns with the understanding that there is an Intelligence receptive to what you are saying that helps you create within your own environment of matter and energy the most effective dynamics to bring you into wholeness."

–GARY ZUKAV *(Thoughts from the Seat of the Soul)*

· I N T E N T I O N ·

This week I will enter into a partnership with Divine Intelligence. I will practice the dynamics of prayer, meditation, visualization, guided imagery, and contemplation. I will use these tools as companions on my Soulwork journey. And so it is.

Acceptance

ACCEPTANCE AND CHANGE

WHAT DOES ACCEPTANCE mean to you? Does it mean a giving up, a giving way, a surrendering? Or does it mean an allowing, a flowing, a letting go and trusting? It has meant both to me over the years. I imagine it is the same for you. One wise teacher, Rabbi Abraham Heschel, tells us that "the higher goal of spiritual living is not to amass a wealth of information, but to face sacred moments." I believe that to be true.

When we begin a year of spiritual discovery, of working with the soul, the logical way to begin is with the quality of action rather than acceptance. We will begin with both, because these two attributes of the soul are needed in equal measure and, paradoxically, at the same time. It is as if you hold two luminous threads in your hands: as you weave them, the inner and the outer, the pushing forward and the letting go, the manifestation and the inner blossoming are woven together so that you cannot tell where one leaves off and the other begins.

When I talk to my wise and loving friends about this book I am writing, the first question they ask me is, "What if I don't want to work in a linear fashion, day by day, week by week? What if I want to dip into a page here and a meditation there? What if I am tired of goals and just want to savor the unexpected insights that come to me as I turn the pages and think on these things?" An echo "What if I just want to face sacred moments?"

Please do. The journey is circular as well as linear. It is miraculous as well as mundane. It is creative as well as disciplinary. There is a sweetness and an awe in working with the qualities of the soul. Your own soul's companion may guide you in a different way than the one in which these essays and meditations are presented. And you may want to start over several times, lingering where you are working through a particular life lesson, skipping an area that does not appeal to you. I would hope that this book would be a joyous and imaginative teacher, one to cherish and return to more than once. I would hope that this book would be a friend, a soulworker's companion, there when needed.

What is more important than the way you use this book is the way in which you accept it. Yes, back to acceptance again! I was taught once that when we want a desired result, first we need an intention or a purpose. You can do that with acceptance as well as action. Then we need to observe, as neutrally as we can, just what is going on in our lives. What stands between us and the desired result we seek? Acceptance of what is works well in this step along our way to positive change. A third step is to look at your mental view of the situation or event, whatever it may be, from a different perspective. I like to go up above the situation to do this, to get a bird's-eye view, so that I can see what action steps to take after I have accepted the whole panorama spread out before me. Then, as a fourth step, I can come back down from the larger, higher view and choose to shift the way I feel about a situation. This too requires the qualities of both acceptance and then action. The fifth and final step in positive and lasting change is to accept that you are now ready to act from the new perspective. You are changed at depth. Some people call this mastery. Some people call this transformation. I call it working with the soul.

The steps we use for our own spiritual development may vary from the ones described above. Prayer changes things. It is a vital part of our pilgrim's progress. Meditation changes things. We become lighter, more discerning, wiser. Ideas and stories change us. We can resonate with the seed thought and find ourselves laughing or crying as the story unfolds. Heart connection changes us. As we open to the relationships around us, we are changed by the needs of the world and we become more loving and more loved.

Acceptance changes things. This is the paradox above all others. I ask you to accept this gift of words, this gift of story, this gift from the heart. Weave your acceptance into each soul lesson. As friends and fellow soulworkers, we'll be companions on the journey.

I invite you to accept this gift.

❧

•INTENTION•

I choose to accept the gifts of the Spirit and the lessons of my heart. I pledge myself to both acceptance and action throughout this year of my soul's discovery. And so it is.

"We begin to realize that there is a sane, awake quality within us. In fact this quality manifests itself only in the absence of struggle. So we discover the Third Noble Truth, the truth of the goal: that is, non-striving. We need only drop the effort to secure and solidify ourselves and the awakened state is present. But we soon realize that just "letting go" is only possible for short periods. We need some discipline to bring us to "letting be." We must walk a spiritual path. Ego must wear itself out like an old shoe, journeying from suffering to liberation."

–CHOGYAM TRUNGPA *(Cutting Through Spiritual Materialism)*

"There is no use in one person attempting to tell another what the meaning of life is. It involves too intimate an awareness. A major part of the meaning of life is contained in the very discovering of it. It is an ongoing experience of growth that involves a deepening contact with reality. . . . The meaning of life cannot be told; it has to happen to a person."

–IRA PROGOFF

Action/Aliveness

FREEING THE ANGEL FROM THE MARBLE

THERE IS A WONDERFUL STORY told of Michelangelo. When asked by his patrons (who paid him to carve and paint) why he was contemplating an amorphous hunk of marble for days instead of working, Michelangelo supposedly responded that he first had to find the perfect form within. Then and only then could he begin to shape the figure. He called this "freeing the angel from the marble."

Each of us has the perfect form within us—our own soul. It is the angel that waits for us to carve away all the beliefs and feelings that have imprisoned us.

In Soulwork, which is our life work, we do not add all that we hope to be onto our outer form. This is not an external journey at all. Instead we find and free the angel caught in the marble. We allow the perfect form to manifest itself through our diligent work of the soul. We will not, of course, then be perfect human beings. We will not have perfect bodies that never age, nor will perfect riches or perfect love shower down upon us. We will, or so I believe, become our own individual, valuable, precious, unique, original, creative, good, true, and beautiful selves.

We will become, through trial and error, through tribulations and hard-won wisdom, through prayerful contemplation and passionate, fulfilling work in the world, through loving and being loved, through giving and receiving, through action and acceptance, become all that our souls desire for us.

We will make a difference in the world.

In this journey, we focus on what we can be. For that reason, this book does not isolate the so-called "negative" emotions of life: rage, resentment, fear, guilt. Healing and using these emotions or energies for good is a lifelong task that is addressed within the intentions and contemplations in this book. They are not set apart to be wrestled with all at once. Since the soul qualities we seek and practice are to be used within everyday life, we do not identify work, family, friendship, or relationship separately. We seek to integrate the inner qualities with our outer lives. We seek to find the invisible form that underlies everything in creation and bring it into the visible world in practical and powerful ways.

This is no grim journey. It can be a joyful pilgrimage, full of prayer and story, full of action and accomplishment. It can be a spiritual adventure. It is our Soulwork. It is our life work. It is our true work.

Sometimes action begins with observing, sorting, and letting go. Sometimes action begins with clearing out and clearing up before outer progress can be discerned. Sometimes action is prayer work. This is tough Soulwork. Wherever you are, you can begin. You have a whole year ahead of you. And a lifetime after that.

What specific actions can I take this week to begin my Soulwork? What specific actions can I take this week in my interactions with others? In my work? In my friendships? In my family or intimate relationships? Do I need to first identify a specific area of my life that is not working and choose a quality of soul that addresses that problem? Or do I need to go within and become quiet and sort out my feelings? Does this week require inner or outer action, or both? Does it require a tiny step or a giant step?

· INTENTION ·

I will ask myself these questions and wait for the still, small voice within to guide me on this year of discovery.

Dear God,

Today is a new beginning. I pledge this day, this week, this month, and this year to spiritual discovery. I will take action as it is revealed to me. I ask for Your help, Your guidance, Your grace in becoming all that I am meant to be. Thank You for Your help. *Amen.*

"Withdraw into yourself and look. And if you do not find yourself beautiful yet, act as does the creator of a statue that is to be made beautiful; he cuts away here, he smoothes there, he makes this line lighter, this other purer, until a lovely face has grown upon his work. So do you also; cut away all that is excessive, straighten all that is crooked, bring light to all that is overcast, labor to make all one glow of beauty and never cease chiseling your statue, until there shall shine out on you from it the godlike splendor of virtue, until you see the perfect goodness surely established in the stainless shrine."

–PLOTINUS

Balance

THE FOURFOLD PERSON

WHEN I WAS YOUNGER and my outside was lovelier than my inside (a situation that has now been reversed), my woman minister told me once that "Balance is beauty." Hmmm. I had never thought of balance in the same breath with beauty. At the time, I was balancing my life among work and school and children and husband and other family members and friends. I juggled and I balanced and I walked gingerly and still I never felt that I got it all right. There was also, in those days, little time for me or for my own quiet balance, my own inner endeavors.

But I remembered what she said. Maybe later, I thought, it will have relevance for me. Later came and I learned that "As above, so below" and "As within, so without." That's balance. I tried my best to live my life with those precepts, sometimes succeeding, sometimes falling short.

Recently I ran across the idea of the "fourfold person" in a tattered copy of *The Twelve Powers of Man* by Charles Fillmore. Actually he called it the "four-square man," but you and I know that we are not rigid squares divided equally, nor are we all male. So I call this idea the four-fold person, because I like to think of all the parts of who we are as banners unfurling in a breeze, spreading our colors in the sky. I like to think of experiencing a freedom and an unwrapping and a floating quality, even as I recognize and explore all that I am. I discovered that for years, without having ever put it into so many words, I had indeed been living the life of the fourfold person. Let me recommend it to you. The fourfold person balances the physical, mental, emotional, and spiritual components of his or her life. That's all! It doesn't take a rocket scientist to understand.

But it does take a commitment to live this way each day. This commitment strives for balance between the mundane issues of everyday life and your increased sensitivity to your inner work. Yes, you work, exercise, and clean your house but you also allow time for quiet contemplation. You learn to balance work and relationships, activity and prayer, the inner and the outer. Where before you may have drowned in emotion and allowed no time for the other three aspects of your life, or perhaps pushed aside your inner life because everyday concerns intruded so insistently, now, little by little, there is a balance between all four aspects of your life.

Yes, it is a balancing act, this task of being in the present as much as possible and paying attention to what is really going on. It is a set of energies interacting in an ever-changing, never-ending dance. It's a process of exquisite calibration.

Living as a fourfold person, full-out, banners flying, puts us in charge. Of all the inner and all the outer, of the within and the without, of the above and the below, of the visible and the invisible, and of the fourfold dance of beautiful, life-enriching balance.

❧

What part of my fourfold person am I neglecting?
The physical? The mental? The emotional? The spiritual?
What steps can I take this week to bring my life into more
balance? If I am engaged in a project that demands
great mental or emotional concentration, can I promise
myself that I will bring my body into balance once current
demands for energy are met? Can I pledge myself to fifteen
minutes of meditation or prayer at the beginning and end
of each day? What promises can I make to myself for
continuing balance throughout this year?

• I N T E N T I O N •

Let me begin now to look at my life as a fourfold person. Let me begin to balance and bring into greater harmony the physical, mental, emotional, and spiritual aspects of

16

myself. I am a fourfold person, dancing in balance. Thank you that this is now so.

· G O A L S ·

I will write down one change I can make this week in order to bring my life into more balance. I will breathe in the word balance with each breath I take. I will breathe out the word balance with each breath I exhale. I will use each opportunity in my life as an opportunity for balance.

"You don't have to suffer continual chaos in order to grow."

–JOHN C. LILLY

"Your power in this life derives not from your ability to produce, but rather from your ability to balance the inflow and out-flow of spirit. And at the root of this ability, your teacher, the breath, moves quietly in and out, automatically regulating and meeting your needs. Observe and listen to this teacher. It will lead you to great harmony."

–ELLEN MEREDITH *(Listening In:*
Dialogues with the Wiser Self)

"Good for the body is the work of the body, and good for the soul is the work of the soul, and good for either is the work of the other."

–HENRY DAVID THOREAU

Dear God,

Please help me to see the changes that need to be made in my life so that I may live a life of balance, physically, mentally, emotionally, and spiritually. As I grow more balanced in my outer life, may I grow more balanced in my inner life and more harmonious in my relationship with You. May I find peace and equilibrium beneath these banners of balance, beneath Your sheltering wings. Thank you that this is now so. *Amen.*

Clarity

LESS IS MORE

W<small>HENEVER</small> I <small>THINK</small> of the soul quality clarity, I think of these marvelous words by the American artist Georgia O'Keeffe: "I decided to start anew—to strip away what I had been taught, to accept as true my own thinking. This was one of the best times of my life. There was no one around to look at what I was doing, no one interested, no one to say anything about it one way or another. I was alone and singularly free, working into my own unknown—no one to satisfy but myself. I began with charcoal and paper and decided not to use any color until it was impossible to do what I wanted to do in black and white. I believe it was June before I needed blue."

Clarity is not about more, more, more. Clarity is about the true, the focused, the exact. It is about stripping everything away until you get to the heart of what you believe, and then adding judiciously, enough to make a pattern that sings. It is about the small and the beautiful, not the large and the grandiose. It is about simplicity, harmony, and purity of line, color, thought, word, deed. Once I wrote a poem about peeling apples. It was a metaphor for clarity. It was a metaphor for life. The last lines read, "Pare the apple to the core/Less is more."

You can, of course, substitute the word creativity for clarity. For surely those of us who make our living by writing and speaking want to be both creative and clear. When I think of clarity it seems to me to be high and pure. It is the color blue, like the clearest of skies after a summer rainstorm, or deep and clear and icy, like a lake that reflects snow-capped mountains in its depths.

Part of my Soulwork has been the task of relinquishing muddy, sloppy, half-formed thoughts and opinions and then searching and finding what I really believe. And for that task, I welcome clarity. It helps me with all my forms of communication. It helps me emotionally as well.

When you begin to think about clarity as a tool, you can make your every act as clear and true and conscious as you can. You can create your life as good, true, and beautiful, no matter the form the clearness takes, whether in singing a song or planting a rosebush, whether in building a church or teaching a child. Contemplation itself can be an exquisite exercise in clarity.

Of course clarity is my writer's tool. It's an inherent goal of mine with every passage I write. Isn't that what Georgia O'Keeffe, who used both the shadows and the blinding light of New Mexico, wanted to express in her work—that clear essence?

When you look at your whole life through the lens of

clarity, then everything you are, everything that you have done, and everything that you will be, is necessary. It is the work of the soul. And the work of the soul is clarity.

How can I become more clear in my thinking this week?
How can I become more clear in my work? How can I
bring the quality of clarity into my relationships?
Into my spiritual life?

· I N T E N T I O N ·

My goal this week is to practice the soul attribute of clarity in all that I think, feel, and do. I affirm that I am becoming clearer, wiser, and more discerning day by day.

"She had opened her mind to the words the way an eye used to darkness, veiled with its lashes, opens cautiously to the light, and, finding it ever a little blinding, closes itself too late. The light had come, and come invincibly, even after the eye had renounced it. It was too late to unsee."

–HANNAH GREEN *(I Never Promised You a Rose Garden)*

"Once in ancient India there was a tournament held to test marksmanship in archery. A wooden fish was set up on a high pole and the eye of the fish was the target. One by one many valiant princes came and tried their skill, but in vain. Before each one shot his arrow the teacher asked him what he saw, and invariably all replied that they saw a fish on a pole at a great height with head, eyes, etc.; but Arjuna, as he took his aim, said, 'I see the eye of the fish,' and he was the only one who succeeded in hitting the mark."

–PARAMANANDA

"The idea is not to become a mere sloth, sitting on your behind with a vacant mind. It is rather to get into the position of being able to concentrate enormously, so that you can, so to speak, look with all your energy—so that you do not miss a thing."

–PAUL WEINPAHL

Dear God,
Please grant me clarity in all that I think, say, feel, and do. I will begin by clearing my mind of all outer busyness, so that I may see the light that You bring into my mind, heart, and soul, and that I may follow that light. Teach me to be a part of Your clear light of truth and beauty. Teach me to see more clearly, live more clearly, and love more clearly. Thank You for clarity. And so it is. *Amen.*

Cleanliness

NEIGHBORHOOD CLEANING LADY

THERE IS A WOMAN who walks by my house almost every morning. She is tailored and efficient. She has short, curly gray hair, and wears khaki shorts with a pink top tucked in crisply and tennis shoes so white I swear she goes home and polishes them every night. I am fascinated by this woman. I call her the neighborhood cleaning lady. She carries a plastic garbage bag with her on her walks. She scoops up the litter on her path. I have seen her right a tricycle that has fallen and set it up on the sidewalk. I have seen her do the same for errant newspapers, sailing them with a thunk to land precisely where they should, on the front porch instead of in the driveway. This morning, as I peered sleepily at her from my dawn perch on my terrace, she took the broken top of a plastic garbage can and placed it with the brush on the other side of the driveway, so that the trash pickup people would not miss it when they came around. Where she passes, not one bottle, can, or cigarette butt remains.

I wonder what her life has been. I see her as a ferocious cleaner of her domain. Perhaps she is a retired secretary, who once kept her boss organized. Perhaps she is a former schoolteacher. Perhaps a homemaker. Now, with children long grown and gone, and probably divorced or widowed (she always walks alone), she has chosen to be the neighborhood litter lady, to extend her well-honed talents outside her home. I expect that when she returns home after her neighborhood policing, she washes her hands three times, sinks down on her couch, and says to herself with a satisfying sigh, "Well, I did my part to clean up the world today."

I wonder what she'd say if I invited her in to help me clean up *my* domain? We could begin with the clutter that multiplies overnight. My paperwork seems to have a mind of its own. Each night it reproduces like rabbits after I go to bed. Oh, the amount of stuff I clear out! I have the best intentions of creating space and light, but only find that there are still more antiques to dust, more laundry to do. I'd like my life to be all neatened up.

When I lived in Los Angeles, eccentricities were common. From street people to movie stars, everyone prided themselves on being different, on being unique, on being self-absorbed. It is not so in this solid, traditional neighborhood in an old-fashioned city in the heart of Texas. In this neighborhood, a throwback to an earlier, gentler time, there is no crime, there are no gangs. The university police patrol my street and those surrounding every fifteen minutes in an endless circle. I feel protected, safe.

It is a benign neighborhood. So if one woman wants to do her part in recycling, wants to neaten up her world, wants to extend herself outside her doorway, wants to tidy up the streets, well then, smile and rejoice. She's doing what she knows best how to do. Create a space of cleanliness and order. More power to her!

Maybe we could enlist an army of middle-aged, industrious women (men too, come to think of it) to clean up the world. They could start with their neighborhoods and move outward in an ever-widening circle, until every neighborhood was scrubbed and shining with order and with care. I've quit laughing at my neighborhood cleaning woman. Some morning I may even join her.

*What can I do this week to clean up the clutter in my life?
What do I need to recycle, reuse, clear out, discard, release?
What are my resistances to tidiness and neatness?
What in my life needs restructuring and order? Can I
extend myself to making some sort of contribution to the
cleanup of my neighborhood? My city? The planet?*

· I N T E N T I O N ·

This week I will make a concentrated effort to put my home, my work, and my personal life in order.

• A F F I R M A T I O N •

Everything in my life is moving toward order, lightness, cleanliness, clarity, space. As I clear out the clutter of my life, I make room for more and more good to come into my life. Everything in my life is in divine order now.

"Fear less, hope more;
Eat less, chew more;
Whine less, breathe more;
Talk less, say more;
Hate less, love more;
And all good things are yours."
–OLD SWEDISH PRAYER

"Strive to be like a well-regulated watch, of pure gold, with open face, busy hands, and full of good works."
–DAVID C. NEWQUIST

Dear God,

I ask for divine order and cleanliness in every area of my thoughts, so that I may be a clear vessel to do Your work and service in the world. Help me to clear away the old chaotic patterns in my life to make room for the new, the good, the true, the beautiful. May I have more space in my life to know and to do Your will. *Amen.*

Compassion

HOW DO YOU CLOSE THE HEART?

ONCE WHEN I WAS ON A LECTURE TOUR in Northern California, two events happened in one day that summed up a lifetime of questioning for me. The first event was a radio interview at 7:30 in the morning. The first question the interviewer asked was, "You write about opening the heart to compassion. Many of us have done that. Now answer this question for our listeners: Once the heart breaks open, how do we close it?"

I was stumped. "Why would you want to?" I ventured over the airwaves.

"Because the pain is too great to bear," the interviewer answered.

"Yes, I know. But I do not know the answer to your question. Once your heart has been broken open, and you have served in whatever capacity you are called upon to serve from that heart center, I do not know how you protect your heart again."

That night, I made a mad dash in the pouring rain through heavy weekend traffic to speak in downtown San Francisco at a church that serves the homeless, runaway teenagers, the ill, the elderly, and people in recovery from addictions. An AIDS ministry is active there, as is hospice.

During a discussion that centered on Soulwork, a similar question was asked of me. "Now that our hearts are broken open in service and in love, how can we go on?"—not "How can we close our hearts?" or "How can we protect ourselves?" but rather, "How can we go on?"

I threw the question back to them. "How do you go on?"

The new minister at the church spoke haltingly of the overwhelming, unending tasks that confronted him daily. "The need is so great, and we are so few." How do you go on?

A young man who had lost a number of his friends to death told of how he often saw people that he knew had passed on, walking the streets of San Francisco. "Sometimes I see them put their hands on people's shoulders; sometimes they just hover quietly in the background." How do you go on?

Some might have dismissed his sightings, or called them ghosts, or wondered at his aberrant mind. But the people in the group nodded in agreement. They knew what he had seen. "They are angels, and they have come back to help the friends who are grieving and who have been left behind. They are angels of compassion."

How do you go on, once your heart has broken open in compassion?

"You can't close up your heart," the group said. "You can only continue living from an open heart. You can only continue serving." How do you go on?

"Why would you want to close up your heart?" they asked. "How much more alive can you be than living with an open heart?" How do you go on?

"You can't close up," they said. "You can't go back to where you were before. You can't unlearn. You can't be ignorant, or live superficially, or meanly, or selfishly. Not ever again." They were adamant. "Not ever again."

When I wrote about my own son's journey, and my family's journey, through life and death in the AIDS crisis, I wrote about tending the wounded, in a never-ending ocean of grief, loss, and pain. I wrote about the lessons I had learned. I wrote about how my life had been changed forever. How do you go on?

"Just as I am a part of all that I have met, I am a part of all that I have written, and I am a part of all that I have mourned. I am a part of all that I have loved. And that's what opening the heart is. To be a part of all that you have ever loved. And to continue loving. At whatever cost."

You cannot close the heart, once it has been broken open. You can only continue loving, at whatever cost, with the hope of angels of compassion at your side. While day by day, and hour by hour, and heartbeat by heartbeat, you go on.

❦

"If you quit loving the moment it becomes difficult, you never discover compassion."

–DAVID AUGSBURGER

Do you quit loving the moment it becomes difficult?
What have you learned from the times in your life
when loving was difficult? How do you go on when
love becomes difficult?

• I N T E N T I O N •

This week I will look at the ways in which I can be more compassionate. This week I will open myself more to other people, attune myself more to their needs, walk a mile or so in their shoes. This week I will pray for more compassion in all that I think, say, and do, including compassion for my self and its unfolding. This week I will have an open heart.

Dear God,

Here I am. I am learning, with Your loving guidance, to look beyond my own, small, selfish needs, to look with compassion on those I come in contact with. I look back at times in my life when I have been ignorant of compassion, and I ask forgiveness for those times of ignorance and uncaring. I no longer want to walk through life with a closed and barricaded heart. I trust in Your compassion as You open my heart, little by little, to compassion for all. Thank You for Your compassion for me and for all those I love. I am grateful. *Amen.*

"God does not comfort us to make us comfortable, but to make us comforters."
                    –JOHN HENRY JARRETT

"The heart that breaks open can contain the whole universe."
                    –JOANNA ROGERS MACY

Congruency

BECOMING REAL

"WHAT IS REAL?" asked the Rabbit. . . . "Real isn't how you are made," said the Skin Horse. "It's a thing that happens to you . . . "

"Does it hurt?" asked the Rabbit.

"Sometimes," said the Skin Horse, for he was always truthful. "When you are Real you don't mind being hurt. . . . It doesn't happen all at once," said the Skin Horse. "You become. It takes a long time. That's why it doesn't often happen to people who break easily, or have sharp edges, or who have to be carefully kept. Generally, by the time you are Real, most of your hair has been loved off, and your eyes drop out and you get loose in the joints and very shabby. But these things don't matter at all, because once you are Real you can't be ugly, except to people who don't understand. . . . [O]nce you are Real you can't become unreal again. It lasts for always."

–MARGERY WILLIAMS *(The Velveteen Rabbit)*

A friend of mine, a psychotherapist who is writing her first book, asked me how it felt to have so many people read and respond to my book *Soulwork.* Maybe she thought I would jump in the air and exclaim "Royalties at last!"

Instead I told her, "It makes me feel visible. In a way I have not felt for years. It makes me feel whole, real, all of a piece. Congruent."

She asked for an explanation. "Oh, I don't mean visible like celebrities are visible," I said. "No one knows what an author looks like, unless they are very, very famous and on all the talk shows. So it's not about being recognized. It's about being real."

"Real?"

"Like in *The Velveteen Rabbit*, where after lots of life experiences and writing about them in an intimate, personal way, people know you. You are visible, you are exposed."

"How scary," she commented.

"Not at all. The scary thing is the next book and the next book and the one after that, where with each page you have to ask yourself, 'Do I really believe this? What do I believe? How can I express this, not only in my writing but in my own life?' It's OK if people don't understand, or judge you, or try to change your mind about what you believe in. It's OK if people want your work to be different, or you to be different. Because then you have the opportunity to say, 'This is who I am. This is what I write. This is what I live. And I am real.'"

My friend, who is a wise and caring woman, helps me, in our long discussions, to see the uniqueness and the universality in each person's life we touch. "It takes a long time to become real," she says. "No wonder that we're often scarred, or some of our stuffing is missing, or we're lumpy, or our joints hurt." We laughed together as only two middle-aged women, who have been through the mill, who have been through the fire, who have been through the dark night of the soul, can. Been there. Done that.

"Don't forget shabby," I cry, quoting the book. "There have been times that we have both been very, very shabby."

"But never poor," she counters. "Always, we have been rich inside."

I know her story. I know how long it has taken her to climb back out of poverty and despair. Great changes have taken place in her life in the last ten years. She lives by faith, not fortune. She's still here.

"A toast," she proclaims. "To us, the richest women in the world."

We clink our iced-tea glasses together and watch the sun go down.

"Because we're real," I echo softly.

"Amen," she says, "and yet again, Amen."

To be congruent means that your outer actions and your inner life match. Thoreau expresses it this way: "As for conforming outwardly, and living your own life inwardly, I do not think much of that."

I don't think much of that either. It is much more restful to drop the mask and be real. And yet it is a challenge as well—to live a congruent life—to be who you are in every area of your life, even while you are changing and growing and discovering all the facets of your miraculous and unique self. But it's the only way I know to become real. Begin now.

Are you living a congruent life? If you are not, in what areas of your life, work, play, family, relationships could you begin to be more real, more visible, more congruent? Where, when, and with whom are you most real? What would it take for you to live both your inner and your outer life in a congruent fashion?

• A F F I R M A T I O N •

I affirm today my own wholeness, harmony, balance. I am real and congruent in every aspect of my life.

"You have everything in you that Buddha has, that Christ has. You've got it all. But only when you start to acknowledge it is it going to get interesting. Your problem is you're afraid to acknowledge your own beauty. You're too busy holding on to your own unworthiness. You'd rather be a schnook sitting before some great man. That fits in more with who you think you are. Well, enough already. I sit before you and I look and I see your beauty, even if you don't."

–RAM DASS *(Grist for the Mill)*

"Do not say things. What you are stands over you the while, and thunders so that I cannot hear what you say to the contrary."

–RALPH WALDO EMERSON

Dear God,

Well, here I am again. Real enough, warts and all. Please help me to see my own wholeness, my own uniqueness. Please help me to see that what I am is enough. Please help me to live my life so that my inner and outer world is in balance, rather than me presenting one face to the world and one face to You. Help me to be real. Thank You. *Amen.*

Courage

OLD BEAR

A FRIEND OF MINE told me this story of courage. Her dad was a strong force in the family legend. He was larger-than-life, a throwback to the days of the western man who died with his boots on. When times got tough, as they did often in the Texas Panhandle region where he lived, he would shake his head and say, "Old Bear can do it. Old Bear will get through." He always referred to himself that way.

My friend explained that her dad was a loving husband and father, a gentleman raised on the harsh prairies, working in the oil fields, a survivor of the Great Depression. "He was a self-made man," she said. "He was a man admired by all."

When her father became ill with heart problems, my friend, an only child, moved him and her mother across hundreds of miles to be closer to her. He had been given only three months to live, and she wanted to help care for him. He moved gratefully, but he also told his wife and daughter, "I'll show that doctor. Old Bear ain't gonna give in. I've got years of good left inside of me." He wanted to see his grandson grow up, and he did. He lived a full, rich life for fourteen more years.

My friend has a number of male cousins who follow in Old Bear's footsteps. When one cousin, getting on in years, was diagnosed with cancer and given only a few months in which to get his affairs in order, the family was devastated. But this is what my friend did. She found letters her father had written when he was ill, and she passed them on to her cousin with her own letter of encouragement and love.

He called her on the phone. "I just keep thinking about Old Bear," he told her. "He never felt sorry for himself. I'm not gonna waste the time I have left in any regrets. I'm gonna be like Old Bear. I'm gonna die when it's my time, as good as he lived. God, the man had courage! I figure Old Bear is just sitting up there somewhere, watching me, helping and hoping that I'll get through this without whining. Yep, Old Bear is watching me. I'll do him proud." My friend's cousin is still alive and kicking.

I can tell you a dozen more stories of solid, stoic people who lived with grace and died with dignity. They are examples of everyday courage. I learn from each of them, from Old Bear to the death of my son Michael.

Sometimes, however, courage is not about a person facing death, or reconsidering his life, or living by his hard-learned gentleman's code of honor. Sometimes courage is just getting up in the morning, instead of giving up. You know that one, don't you?

Sometimes courage is about caregivers. Here's what Lon Nungesser wrote in *Axioms for Survivors:* "A hospice social worker once said to me that death was much harder on the living than on the dying."

I know the path of caregiving. I honor the continuing courage of the everyday heroes on that path.

When I look around me, I see countless tales of courage. The single mother in her forties who is raising a toddler alone. The single parent of three teenagers who is starting her own business. The mother who cares for her handicapped child and the other members of her family. The artist who pushes through barriers of self-imposed and societal limitations in order to create something beautiful. The man who stands up with the courage of his convictions. I see heroes everywhere.

Old Bear didn't spend a lot of time wondering if he had done something wrong because this calamity had fallen upon him. Neither did his cousin. He didn't spend a lot of time bewailing his fate. He just got on with it. He died as he had lived, with courage.

You live with courage too. I know you do. You are the hero of your own life as am I of mine.

Wonder what courage has waiting around the bend for us? Maybe Old Bear knows. We'll come through.

❧

I discovered this prayer about ten years ago. The author is unknown. It is a magnificent example of Native American spirituality and courage.

Oh Great Spirit, whose voice I hear in the winds,
    and whose breath gives life to all the world.
Hear me.
I come before you one of your many children.
I am small and weak. I need your strength and
    wisdom.
Let me walk in beauty. Make my eyes ever to behold
    the red and purple sunset.
Make my hands respect the things you have made—
    my ears sharp to hear your voice.
Make me wise, so that I may know the things you have
    taught my people—the lesson you have hidden in
    every rock.
I seek strength—not to be superior to my brothers—
    but that I may be able to fight my greatest enemy—
    myself.
Make me ever ready to come to you with clean hands
    and straight eyes.
So that when life fades, as a fading sunset, my spirit
    can come to you without shame.

–PRAYER OF A CHIEF OF THE DAKOTA SIOUX

How courageous are you? How do you meet life—with
fear and trembling or with strength and fortitude?
Think of someone who exemplifies courage to you.
Can you live up to his or her level of courage?

• I N T E N T I O N •

I am becoming a strong and courageous human being.

"It costs so much to be a full human being that there are very few who have the enlightenment or the courage to pay the price. . . . One has to abandon altogether the search for security, and reach out to the risk of living with both arms. One has to embrace the world like a lover. One has to accept pain as a condition of existence. One has to court doubt and darkness as the cost of knowing. One needs a will stubborn in conflict, but apt always to total acceptance of every consequence of living and dying."

–MORRIS L. WEST *(The Shoes of the Fisherman)*

"Courage is the price life exacts for granting peace."
–AMELIA EARHART

Creativity and Divine Order

PULLING CLOUDS

WHAT EXACTLY DOES CREATIVITY have to do with order? Everything. Here is what Carl Jung said about order. I use his words often to focus my mind so that I can concentrate and become more creative in my work. "Whereas I formerly believed it to be my bounden duty to call other persons to order, I now admit that I need calling to order myself."

Like Carl Jung, I often feel like I need calling to order myself. As I grow older, I yearn for order in every aspect of my life, from my files to my creativity to my closets to my relationships. One of my favorite phrases to repeat to myself whenever I am overextended in any or all areas of my life is "Divine Order." I've had to learn Divine Order the hard way, as I tend to see the big picture and let God worry about the details.

Currently I am writing a book for one publisher, compiling and editing another book for a second publisher, and publicizing a third book for yet another publisher. Every writer's dream. Be careful what you ask for. You may get it all at once! I also have people in my life who are important to me and need tending like a well-watered garden. So there's not much time for clutter and disorder in my life.

When my life feels as crowded as it does now, I tend to try to do everything at once. Not a great idea where creativity is involved, when long blocks of time, on a consistent basis, are required, and where dreaming and thinking play as integral a part in composition as time spent at the computer.

A wise editor once told me that "reorganization is insight." Well yes, and that phrase has helped me in the nitty-gritty of tearing down pages and rebuilding them from scratch. But what do you do when you don't have time for reorganization? You reorganize your time.

It seems to me that there is an expanding part of creativity and a contracting part of creativity. Just like life. There are times you have to sweep everything out of the way, in order for the still small voice to whisper to you and give you stories and insights to share with others. And there is the time when one word at a time has to be inserted on a scrolling screen, form a pattern and a rhythm, and then, be corrected and smoothed and shaped into—what else?—order.

Recently an image came to me of just what this process of creativity flowing—sometimes forced!—into form looks like. I see that I am pulling clouds through a thermometer. There is the catching on to clouds and the going down with them, and the form they must be fitted into, and the going up again with the clouds packed firmly into the thermometer, and all rising until the correct temperature is reached. A going down and a rising up. Packing the inner into the outer and the outer into the inner receptacle. It's been a marvelous help to me to see the process of creativity this way. To create a form to hold the clouds of thought. Maybe you can use this analogy in the work you do. Maybe it will help you with your organization or reorganization. I hope so.

And when all else fails, try repeating the phrase "Divine Order" like a mantra night and day. That helps too. Because, whether you are creating books or pulling clouds through a thermometer, creativity and order go hand in hand.

"When you listen to me, when you read me, you do not merely give me your attention and your time; you give me part of your most precious possession: your life. My communication with you must therefore be as precious as your life."

–ROBERT MULLER *(A Planet of Hope)*

"I do not sit down at my desk to put into verse some-thing that is already clear in my mind. If it were clear in my mind, I should have no incentive or need to write about it. . . . We do not write in order to be understood; we write in order to understand."

– C. DAY LEWIS *(The Poetic Image)*

"On a hot day in the southern desert of Africa I had wanted to go and speak to one of my favorite Stone Age Hunters. He was sitting in the middle of a thorn bush. . . . He was huddled in an attitude of the most intense concentration . . . but his friends would not let me get near him, saying, 'But don't you know, he is doing work of the utmost importance. He is making clouds.' "

– LAURENS VAN DER POST

Devotion

GOD HAS NEED OF YOUR PRAYERS

ONCE, WHEN SOMEONE I LOVED was going through a difficult time, I talked to a minister friend of mine at great length about the tragedy. She said something to me that I thought, at the time, was very curious. She said, "I know you pray to God about this situation. Do not forget that God has need of your prayers also."

God has great need of your prayers. Whatever your personal relationship with the God of your being, it is not a one-way street. We have for centuries been supplicants, begging God to heal us, to save us, to give to us. But God has great need of our prayers also. When we ask for strength, it is to be the work of God's hands. When we ask for more understanding, it is to be the work of God's mind. When we ask to be more loving, it is to be the work of God's heart. God works through us, not just to us.

In the little prayer song I wrote for *Soulwork*, I wrote about opening the heart. I sing this song to myself each day during my early-morning walks:

Open my heart, that I may see
Visions of good You have for me.

Open my heart, that I may hear
Your love and wisdom guiding me clearly.

Open my heart, that I may feel,
All that is true, all that is real.

Open my heart, that I may know,
What I must do and where I must go.

Open my heart, that I may be
Whatever, in love, You want me to be.

Recently a new friend called me. She had read my book and wanted to use the open the heart prayer in one of her sermons. She is a Methodist minister in a small town. I was touched that the words I wrote would be shared in that context. As I was writing this passage, she called me to tell me that she had invited the entire congregation to use the "Open My Heart" prayer as a daily meditation for one year. Later she gave me a copy of the pastoral prayer that she wrote and spoke to her congregation, using the same theme of opening the heart. The words and the devotion behind the words have come full circle. Now I can share with you her prayer.

Devotion takes many forms. When we open our hearts and ask how we can be of use to God, the open hands and open hearts we offer create a circle of shared devotion. Then we are of value to God, a co-creator instead of merely being a supplicant. Energy shared, energy recirculated, energy multiplied.

God has great need of your prayers.

❦

Open Heart Prayer

"Oh God,

We come here this morning hoping to be refreshed here in worship like a summer rain refreshes the hard, dry ground. We are reminded that the soft drops of water can wear away the hardest stone. Let Your love be like drops of water which wear away our hearts of stone.

Show us a way into the cave of our heart to listen to our heart's song. Listen to our heart's song which will never forget us. Never forsake us. Let us be tender-hearted and open-hearted. Let us trust in an open heart. In Thy Name. *Amen.*"

–PRAYER BY THE REVEREND SANDRA J. LYDICK

Am I an open-hearted person? What are the occasions and who are the people around which I close up my heart? Do I believe that others have need of my prayers? Do I act on that belief? What can I do for others? Is it possible that God has need of my prayers? What can I do for God?

• G O A L •

I will remember and meditate on the following words this week.

"The way from God to a human heart is through a human heart."

–S. D. GUADAN

I will use the Open My Heart passage every day for one week as a walking meditation as I go about my daily tasks.

• I N T E N T I O N •

May I be an open-hearted, tender-hearted, wide-hearted, loving-hearted person this week and in the weeks to come. And so it is.

"I knew that if God loved me, then I could do wonderful things, I could try great things, learn anything, achieve anything. For what could stand against me with God, since one person, any person with God, constitutes the majority?"

–MAYA ANGELOU (Wouldn't Take Nothing for
My Journey Now)

Endurance/Fortitude

LOOKING FOR TRANSFORMATION

ONCE WHEN I WAS VISITING New York City, I went to a breakfast meeting with some people in publishing I knew slightly, although they were not my publishers, and I was not a part of their meeting. I knew enough to be the proverbial fly on the wall during their discussions.

I love publishing and talks of deals and contracts and subsidiary rights generally thrill me down to my toes. But I was distracted. I was watching the shoes of the waitress who served us. I knew her feet hurt by the way she walked, the way her ankles fell outward over the orthopedic type shoes she wore. I could almost feel the bunions straining under the leather. It was only eight-thirty in the morning, and she would probably walk twenty thousand steps or more during the course of the day. But only her feet spoke of her suffering: She was efficient, swift, with an economy of motion that suggested a ballet dancer instead of a middle-aged, overweight woman serving others all day.

"Thank you!" I said to her politely each time she brought us something. "Thank you very much." She looked surprised, as if the brusqueness of New York had inured her to the possibility of receiving thanks. She smiled at me, a swift smile that lit up her whole face. While the men talked on, I made up an entire story of her life, starting with how her feet hurt and why she had to take this job. For a moment it was as if I saw into the pattern of her life, its problems, and the continuing endurance she had to muster in order to meet each day. I knew about the ex-husband in prison, the married daughter who wanted her to baby-sit on the weekends (when all she wanted to do was put up her feet), and the elderly aunt who required increasing time and care and part of her paycheck to survive.

The businessmen were talking about signing a book contract with a man who had gone through a spontaneous transformation process years before and the possibilities of a bestseller, although they concluded, "He's a lousy writer and a terrible public speaker."

"Then why," I ventured to say, my attention caught, "would you want to publish him?"

"Everybody's looking for transformation," was the reply. "And this is the real thing, the genuine article."

"Wait!" I protested. "We're all in the process of transformation, aren't we? Why *this* man? I don't understand."

They went on talking as if I didn't exist. I caught the waitress' eye. She grinned at me, gave me a wink so fleet I almost missed it, and then refilled the cups all around. I grinned back, woman to woman. We knew.

When I lived in Santa Monica, California, there was a somewhat cynical saying that there was a guru on every street corner. A smorgasbord of redemption and reinvention awaited those who, thirsty for knowledge and adrift in the big city, paid big bucks for a glimpse of a more hopeful future and the chance to huddle with like-minded people in a hotel ballroom where your future would be magically transformed. I know. I was there.

Where I live now, there are six—count them, six!—cable channels devoted to evangelists, airwave preachers who exhort, in an old-fashioned, Bible-thumping oratory, that to follow them and to give them money, lots and lots of money, is the way to inherit the keys to the kingdom. In fact, every time I turn on the television, there is someone—politician, preacher, or personality—who will tell me how to be saved or how to be found.

I am not lost. There is nothing I need saving from. There is no earthly intermediary who will lead me to the promised land. Although, of course, I still learn from good books and good speakers, I learn more from friends and family. I learn from direct experience. I learn from a waitress whose feet hurt. To paraphrase a famous saying, "Transformation, like old age, ain't for sissies."

I think that I, you, we, are all transformers. More than flesh and bone, we are energy systems, with a spark of the

Divine within each of us. One task is to contact and connect with that spark within, nurture it in hope and faith, and give it back into the world. Another task is to recognize that spark of light in our fellow human beings and to honor it, whatever our gifts may be—whether gifts of words, or gifts of waitressing.

Everybody's looking for transformation. Look then, for the Divine within the ordinary. Look for the wisdom within each individual. Look for the holy in the daily. Everybody's looking for transformation. Everybody's doing it.

Do I tend to judge others by their outward appearance?
Do I equate success, whether material or spiritual, with a
person's age, gender, or profession?

• INTENTION •

This week I will look for the holy in the daily. I will look within the soul of each person I meet, to see their beauty and their gifts of transformation.

"It is one thing to go through a crisis grandly, but another thing to go through every day glorifying God when there is no witness, no limelight, no one paying the remotest attention to us."

–OSWALD CHAMBERS

"Each human being is a prism in which the whole universe is reflected."

–ROBERT MULLER *(A Planet of Hope)*

Faith

WHERE GOD COMES IN

IT'S TAKEN ME A LONG TIME to get back to nature. Somehow city canyons are not conducive to the slow pace of meditative walking. Everybody's hurrying, hurrying, hurrying. Can I even catch my breath in a world full of instant results, instant success?

No, I can't. While I am landlocked now—far from the ocean I once walked by, back in those days where only sea-dividing horizon and setting sun rippling toward me across the water were enough to comfort me—now, at least, I have time. Time to reflect and time to savor. Time to stroll.

Past the midpoint in my life, even though I intend to live a long, long time, I've come at last to that most lovely line from Wordsworth which echoes through me, "Emotion recollected in tranquillity." That's what a poem is, you know: "Emotion recollected in tranquillity." That, of course, is what life is too. That is, if we are very lucky and a little wise, and can reflect on where we have been, and make conscious choices in the now.

Everybody's recycling these days. I am too. I'm recycling emotion, recollecting it in tranquillity, creating a purpose and a meaning for my past. I'm collecting and re-cycling words too, those varied and almost infinite arrangements of ideas, syllables, and sounds, that evoke emotion within me, that trigger response.

I began writing when I was six years old. I used to watch the leaves and the light on the leaves of the tree that soared past the upstairs window of the old Victorian house I lived in, where, with all my books and all my thoughts and a tablet of writing paper, I would crouch on the velvet pew cushions of the built-in window seat, and then—wonder of wonders!—dream my way into "the way the leaves must feel."

I was sixteen when I wrote a poem about those specific, rustling, alive leaves. I said, "There are spaces between the leaves where God comes in." The poem was published, along with some others. I have not thought of it for years—until today. Until today, scuffling through autumn leaves that drift in choruses of yellow, orange, rust. That drift me backwards into a time when I knew, without a shadow of a doubt, that "there are spaces between the leaves where God comes in."

Perhaps memory is a way to recycle faith. To seize the ecstatic instant, whether dreaming in a window seat or striding through autumn leaves. To know, to believe. To recapture, to recollect. To be both tranquil and joyful. To be as alive as the leaves of long ago and the leaves that cover and christen your shoes as you walk, remembering.

One with the leaves and the spaces between the leaves where God comes in.

Dear God,

With Your loving encouragement, I will look for faith in every flower, plant, tree, or leaf. I will look for faith in the spaces between the leaves and the sun shining through the leaves. I will rejoice in the evidence of faith reborn in nature. I will see Your handiwork reflected in the world around me. I will remember and be blessed. And so it is. *Amen.*

"Every moment and every event of every man's life plants something in his soul. For just as the wind carries thousands of winged seeds, so each moment brings with it grains of spiritual vitality that come to rest imperceptibly in the minds and wills of men. Most of these unnumbered seeds perish and are lost, because men are not prepared to receive them. For such seeds as these cannot spring up anywhere, except in the good soil of freedom, spontaneity, and love."

–THOMAS MERTON

"What keeps our faith cheerful is the extreme persistence of gentleness and humor. Gentleness is everywhere in daily life, a sign that faith rules through ordinary things: through cooking and small talk, through storytelling, making love, fishing, tending animals and sweet corn and flowers, through sports, music, and books, raising kids— all the places where the gravy soaks in and grace shines through . . . "

–GARRISON KEILLOR

Fidelity

BEING FAITHFUL

WHERE DO FIDELITY AND LOYALTY START? It seems to me that they are as much about a person's character and a person's convictions as about being faithful to a certain ideal or goal or person. I remember what a family friend said about one of my sons, as he helped his brother while his brother lay dying. "You know, John knows just exactly who he is. He's not out searching for his identity or questioning what he believes in. He's just himself. And he's restful to be around."

I think that we grow into our character. We grow into our convictions. We decide what we believe in. And then we live by those beliefs. When I think about loyalty or fidelity I think of more than fidelity to a spouse or loyalty to one's country. I think about how we live our lives, not what we say about how we live our lives. Before this turns into a sermon, I would like to say that I wrestled long and hard with these ideas. In the course of a lifetime, very few of us can say, "I always did everything right." Of course not! We may walk away from bad marriages, we may fail at business, we may live part of our lives in selfishness, ignorance, or addiction. There are no saints among us.

But it's what we do with the continuing moral choices that we face that determines whether our soul is starved and shocked and shivering, or blossoming into its destiny.

I have done the things I ought not to have done, and I have not done the things I should have done. Haven't you? Haven't we all? And now where am I? Choosing once again. Choosing love instead of hate. Kindness instead of selfishness. Courage instead of fear. Creativity instead of rigidity. Tolerance instead of contempt. Choosing fidelity to the best within me instead of being unfaithful to myself. Choosing loyalty to my highest dreams and goals instead of being disloyal to the best and the brightest within me. Keeping my agreements. Giving my word. Forgiving my mistakes.

Your fidelity or loyalty or convictions may look very different from mine. You may espouse a cause I don't believe in, stand on the opposite side of me concerning a political issue, choose a way of life that seems incomprehensible to me, worship or not worship in a different context than what I believe. But do you live your loyalties? Are you congruent with your beliefs? Does your inner and outer life match? Above all, are you faithful to yourself? These are the questions to ask yourself, as I have asked them of myself. By asking yourself questions about your values, your belief systems, and then living your truth, you become whole, instead of living with divided loyalties at war within and a chaotic life without.

Then—thank God!—you're more restful to be around.

❦

"The self is not something ready-made, but something in continuous formation through choice of action."

–JOHN DEWEY

"I can only say I have acted upon my best convictions, without selfishness or malice, and by the help of God I shall continue to do so."

–ABRAHAM LINCOLN

"Some things you must always be unable to bear. Some things you must never stop refusing to bear. Injustice and outrage and dishonor and shame. No matter how young you are or how old you have got. Not for kudos and not for cash. Your picture in the paper nor money in the bank, neither. Just refuse to bear them."

–WILLIAM FAULKNER

"Always do what's right. It will gratify half of mankind and astound the other."

–MARK TWAIN

Dear God,

Help me to be loyal and faithful to myself as well as to others. Strengthen my character and my convictions so that, whether in the darkness or in the light, my actions lead only to good. Thank You. *Amen.*

w e e k   f i f t e e n

Forgiveness

SEVEN STEPS TO FORGIVENESS

Whenever I do readings from *Soulwork*, the most requested story is called "Throwing Stones." It's about the specific physical steps you can take to overcome and release your resentments. In other words, it's about forgiveness.

I've written stories about forgiveness and poems about forgiveness and exercises about forgiveness and chapters about forgiveness. I've written about forgiveness in more books than you can count on the fingers of one hand. You'd think I'd be an expert on the subject by this time, wouldn't you?

Yet when I spoke at an inner-city church in San Francisco, a man asked me, in the discussion that followed, "Where are you in your soul process? Where are you, right now, on your soul path?" And like a stammering stuttering schoolgirl, all I could think to answer was, "Well, I'm still working on forgiveness." Aren't we all? What else is new?

I guess that God was trying to tell me something. Three days after I returned home from that lecture trip, I was asked to write a book on forgiveness. A whole book.

Thanks! I needed that!

In the course of writing *Journey Toward Forgiveness,* I dug deeper and deeper into the ground of my being, questioning, observing, practicing forgiveness. Since I can only write what I believe in, this was a magnificent and synchronistic opportunity—there are no accidents in the universe!—for me to discover just what forgiveness is and is not, and then to come up with a plan for practicing this most maligned and misunderstood soul quality.

"Seven Steps to Forgiveness" unfolded in perfect order before me. I wrote them down. I used these steps in meditation and in my daily life at every opportunity. I practiced them diligently until there was no one left to forgive. Not even God. Not even me. I will continue to use them, even as new challenges and choices arise.

Seven Steps to Forgiveness

I. RECOGNITION AND ACKNOWLEDGMENT
We recognize a problem, situation, event, relationship, or emotion that alerts us to the need to forgive. We acknowledge the problem, situation, event, relationship, or emotion that needs forgiveness.

2. DESIRE, DEFINITION, AND DECISION
We desire to forgive. We define the parameters of the

problem, situation, event, relationship, or emotion. We then make a clear and conscious decision to forgive.

3. MEDITATION AND PRAYER

We go within and with prayerful inquiry and an open, receptive mind, we ask for truth, help, and guidance in the forgiveness situation. We ask how best to proceed to heal the problem, situation, event, relationship, or emotion requiring forgiveness.

4. INNER AND OUTER ACTION

We act on the guidance we have received in prayer and meditation. We do what needs to be done to clear up the problem, situation, event, relationship, or emotion that requires forgiveness.

5. SURRENDER AND RELEASE

After taking appropriate action in the outer world, we release the entire situation into the hands of our Creator. We ask for the highest good of all concerned. We ask, "Thy will, not mine, be done."

6. UNDERSTANDING AND AWARENESS

We look for an increased understanding of the dynamics that led to the problem, situation, event, relationship, or emotion that required our forgiveness. We look for the spiritual lesson. We determine to go forward in forgiveness with increased awareness.

7. HEALING AND CHANGE

We accept that the situation has now changed. We accept that the lesson has been learned. We choose to look at the situation and the world differently. We welcome healing and change through the process of forgiveness. We allow the energy of healing and change to spill over into other areas of our lives. We are changed. We give thanks.

Even as I am reading the Seven Steps to Forgiveness, I feel their potency as a gift to me and from me. They are an ongoing part of my Soulwork. And so I encourage you to take the steps into your heart and mind and use them in whatever way that is needed for you on your soul journey at this time. I ask you to forgive.

*Who do you need to forgive most here and now, today?
Are you willing to forgive that person, once and for all,
totally and without reservation? If so, follow the Seven Steps
to Forgiveness. If not, ask these questions. When will you be
willing to forgive? What will it take for you to forgive?
Are you willing to let the soul within you be the agent of
forgiveness? Are you willing to allow the God of your being
to help you to forgive? Ask all these questions and more,
until you can forgive.*

"Allow yourself to pray. Just as the many times human beings find themselves in circumstances where the hurt or the pain is so great that on their own power they cannot forgive, it is enough that they pray to be given the grace, the perception, the elevated Light that will allow them to forgive."

–GARY ZUKAV *(Thoughts from the Seat of the Soul)*

Frugality

THE SMOCKED BIRTHDAY DRESS

I'M WRAPPING A PRESENT for my mother's seventy-ninth birthday. This afternoon I'll take it to the nursing home where she has lived since she has been unable to take care of herself. I'm glad I found it, after searching for weeks. There's so little I can give her, besides my presence, and there's so much I'd like to give. It's a dress, navy-blue and white-dotted swiss cotton, with the yoke smocked in white flowers. You have to be careful what you buy her. Everything has to button down the front (to be easy to get in and out of), be washable and noncrushable. It must be a dress instead of a "lounge coat" (she abhors those), and it must be a pretty, becoming color. And, oh yes, it must be very, very small. I found a pink dress almost like this one two years ago and bought it for her birthday then. She wears loves it. I've been looking for a similar one since.

I went to her favorite store, the one I remember best by the terrible day that she cried and I got angry. I had taken her to the beauty shop. I had also taken her to the drugstore, the post office, the grocery store. I had taken her to brunch. She wanted then to go shopping. I resisted. I was tired and cranky and so was she. She began to cry. I was so frustrated that I wanted to drop her at her doorstep and go on. Instead, we went to her favorite store, and I took her hand and walked her through the crowds. I could see that she was bewildered and confused. We bought nothing. I took her home at last. I was the one who cried then, all the way home—tears of sadness and anger at the cruel disease which was diminishing my once strong and capable mother.

The store is now going out of business. The only—I swear the only!—dress not on sale was the one I am wrapping now. I paid full price. There is a joke in our family about the time that a friend of mine gave my mother a closetful of clothes she had outgrown. This was years ago, and my mother was working and busy and as always, wistfully frugal. She wanted the best and paid the least, and wished it were different. Some of the blouses my friend gave my mother still had their tags on them. She picked one up, saw the price, and dropped it in horror. "How can I wear this?" she exclaimed. "To pay so much for a blouse. It's wicked. Wicked, wicked, wicked." The blouse cost $50. For years I could not spend more than $50 on an item of clothing. My mother's chant echoed through my brain. "It's wicked. Wicked, wicked, wicked."

But I pay full price for the dress. She will wear it once

or twice, for her birthday or for the church services held at the nursing home—on the days that she is able to remember them and able to attend in a wheelchair.

When I saw the dress, I immediately thought of the smocked and embroidered dresses that my mother made for me when I was a child. She would pin the cotton dress goods on a chair back, anchor it, and with precise and loving stitches, she would hand-embroider the yoke of each of my dresses. She would wash (by hand) and starch and iron the dresses too. I always had a row of them to put on, fresh and waiting.

There is a time for living and a time for dying, a time for spending and a time for saving. Today is not a day for frugality. Today is a day for balloons and birthday cards and cake and ice cream, and new dresses bought full price from my mother's favorite store, where she can no longer go on outings. Maybe I can find slippers to match. That would be a treat. What matters is the gift. And the gift is good, good, good.

When and how do you practice thrift and frugality? When and how do you decide when frugality is not required? Is your frugality flexible, according to the situation? Can you be both generous and frugal?

O Holy Spirit,
I want so very much to be a loving and generous person.
There are times in my life when I have had to be very
frugal, in order to survive. I have learned thrift and care-
fulness and the wise use of money. Yet there are times
when full-out generosity is a wiser use of what I have to
give. Help me to see that there is always enough and
more than enough to act out of kindness and love. And
so it is. *Amen.*

"Taken separately, the experiences of life can work harm
and not good. Taken together, they make a pattern of
blessing and strength the likes of which the world does
not know."

–V. RAYMOND EDMAN

"I am convinced both by faith and experience that to
maintain one's self on the earth is not a hardship but a
pastime—if we live simply and wisely."

–HENRY DAVID THOREAU

Generosity

BREAD

"If you've not been fed, be bread."
–JELALUDDIN RUMI

I REMEMBER A NIGHT LAST SPRING. After a long and tiring plane trip across the country, I had arrived for a lecture tour and was staying with a professional colleague who was also a friend. We enjoyed a late lunch together, some meetings and errands, and so decided to skip supper. I was exhausted. My mother's then-three-year illness had taken its toll on me. I was under financial and professional pressures as well. All I wanted was a hot bath, a book, and some sleep.

"Are you hungry?" she asked. Yes, I was, although it was very late by my jet-lag clock. Despite my feeble protestations that I really didn't need anything to eat, she busied herself in the kitchen with pots and pans. Soon the enticing smells of peppery, garlicky sauce drifted out to the living room.

We ate at the kitchen counter. Handmade pottery bowls were filled with pasta and homemade sauce. I bent over my bowl so that she would not see my tears. I wanted to lay my head down on the kitchen counter and weep. It had been so long since someone—anyone!—had given to me, had fed me. I wanted to spill my heart out, my fears, my grief, my longing to be understood, to be comforted, to be soothed. I didn't. We were just finding our way back to a professional friendship. I didn't want to scare her with my woes. I ate with gusto. I savored every bite. I took the meal in with all my senses. I said "thank you" and fled to my room, dissolving into private tears.

If you have been fed, be bread.

A month earlier, a new acquaintance of mine, a woman who had read my books, came into my life. We had a lot in common and decided to meet at her apartment for tea and talk. When she opened the door, I saw a table set with china and flowers. She began to sing: "Happy birthday to you! Happy birthday to you!" She had fixed me a surprise birthday dinner. She flung out her arms with joy at her surprise. We hugged each other in laughter. Then she fed me. She has become one of my dearest friends.

If you have been fed, be bread.

My best friend for a number of years is as busy as I am. She runs her own company, and gives and gives and gives to everyone. She is much loved. She held my shaking hands when I returned from my seven years sojourn working in the AIDS crisis in Los Angeles. She listened.

She helped put me back together. We meet mostly for meals, since we are both so busy. We've solved a lot of problems breaking bread together. I know that I could call her in the middle of the night and she would meet me at the hospital, during the emergencies that beset my mother. She would watch with me through the night. And then she would feed me.

There have been many times in my life when I have not been fed. When I have given and given and given even when I felt starved inside. So it is a good saying, "If you've not been fed, be bread." But there comes a time when we need to receive. We need to fill up with friendship. We need to be nourished by others. We need to be fed ourselves. Unstintingly, we need to be fed.

Because of the nurturing I have received from my dear women friends, caring and compassion offered in the ritual of food offered and food shared, I can fill up the starved and stoic places within me. Then I can visit my mother, opening my arms to her, holding her trembling frame within my strong and resolute arms. And with hands outstretched, I can bring her food. I can feed her.

If you have been fed, be bread.

I am bread.

• I N T E N T I O N •

I will be bread to others and accept bread for myself in all that I think, say, and do.

Dear God,

Thank You for the gift of generosity. How many times in my life You have given and given and given to me, and then helped me to learn to give to others! I can both give and receive. I can both feed others and be fed. As You are bread to me, so can I be bread to others. Thank You for Your Grace. And so it is. *Amen.*

"Around the table of death and life, bread and wine, where we can still meet each other, there are sounds to hear if we listen carefully. There is the sound of going down into the abyss and being lifted up, heart and body, not to heaven but to the good earth. There are the sounds of the lively ghosts of God, laughing still with love. There are the sounds of men and women stirring, standing. There is the sound of the seasons' changing. And wine. There is the sound of the day breaking. And bread."

–JAMES CARROLL

Goodness

ARE YOU GOOD ENOUGH?

A FRIEND OF MINE, a woman in her fifties, is still struggling with the heritage of a rigid, bitter, controlling mother. She's a therapist, so she works with a lot of people with the same issues. One day she told me that she was going to write a book. Its title would be "Enoughness."

"I'm not into blame or shame," she told me, "but oh how I would like to feel, someday, that I am good enough just the way I am."

Wouldn't we all? No matter what our childhood conditioning was, who hasn't had a taste of "you're not good enough" or "you don't do enough for me" or "if only you could be prettier, thinner, smarter, sweeter, different, more like your sister, less like your father," and onward in a never-ending spiral of "if onlys."

Of course this is standard, basic, classic therapeutic fare. You've heard it. So have I. Forgive your parents, learn to love yourself, make your own way in a world that judges differences more harshly than any childhood echoes.

So when you begin the work of the soul, it is no wonder that you may often feel like the distance between who you are now (or think you are) and who you want to be then, is widening with every step you take.

But Soulwork isn't about a new and improved version of you. Soulwork is you being you. And you are good. Maybe you just need a reminder every now and then. You are a good person. You are good enough. You don't have to meet some impossible standard of perfection. You don't have to please the world or the ghosts of your ancestors.

Goodness cannot be stereotyped. It flowers out of you in unexpected ways. When you're least noticing. When you're least judging. When you get off your own back.

I like the idea of "enoughness." I can take it and apply it to more than the rare inner contentment that comes when I've quit striving and trying and judging. I can say and mean, "I am enough. I have enough. I do enough." I can apply it to projects and money and time and love.

And my friend? She continued with her quest for inner acceptance and "enoughness." It must have worked. What an amazing transformation! She recently moved back into her original home, the one she had leased for two years to others when she didn't have enough money to live there. She's started her own holistic healing center. She's teaching college. She's lost a lot of weight, after a decade of struggle. And recently a wonderful man has come into her life.

She hasn't written her book yet. She's living it instead. She must have done something right.

❧

In what ways do you judge yourself for not being good enough? Write them down.
How can you change these messages? Write down three things you can do this week to feel good about yourself.

• I N T E N T I O N •

I choose to remember that I am enough, I have enough, I do enough. I'm good enough right now.

Dear Higher Self,
You have been with me through all the days of my life. You have encouraged me, helped me, loved me without judgments. Please continue to remind me of my own inherent goodness. As I see the goodness within others, so may I also recognize it within myself. Thank you for Your help. And so it is. *Amen.*

"Cannot we let people be themselves, and enjoy life in their own way? You are trying to make another you. One is enough."

–RALPH WALDO EMERSON *(Self Reliance)*

Gratitude

SAYING YES TO LIFE

LET ME TELL YOU ABOUT GRATITUDE. I believe that if every day we began to thank God, others, and ourselves for every single thing we see around us, it would change our lives. Thank you, thank you, thank you, thank you, thank you we could write, and chant, and sing, and speak aloud and in the silence. Thank you. With every breath. Breathing in God. Breathing out thank you. Would there be room then for guilt, for anger, for resentment, for fear? Sometimes. But the very act of expressing gratitude in the daily can help us when the daily turns to despair.

There is a time to sit down, with a trusted counselor or friend, or in solitude and prayer, and wrestle with the unhealed, despairing sorrows of the heart. This is a necessary task, and one that cannot be rushed. A great part of the kindness you can extend to yourself is to take these times for healing. Feel the feelings. Express your pain. Ask for solutions. Expect healing. But there have been times in my life when I drowned in my emotions. When they took me over, flattened me, dissolved me, threw me into a dark well. I climbed out. I honored my emotions. And I kept on going.

Lately, however, I have begun to see that as I grow stronger in the other areas of my fourfold being, stronger physically and mentally and certainly spiritually, that the emotions don't always have to take me on such a roller-coaster ride. This once felt like heresy to me, because years of learned suppression of emotions took their toll, and I had to learn to release the emotions and to work with their energy, instead of fighting them. It's a necessary and important step, not to be rushed, not to be ignored, not to be missed.

And now? And now I am learning to ride the emotions, instead of being swept out to sea by them. To know that "This too shall pass" and "Tomorrow it will indeed look different." I am learning not only to honor and express my emotions but to put them into perspective. I have emotions, but I am not my emotions.

One of the ways I do this is with an attitude of gratitude. Yes, this hurts. Yes, this seems unsolvable. Yes, this seems to go on forever. How can I bear this? And this? And this? In spite of all this, there are people, places, things, and yes, even emotions I can be thankful for—not by controlling my emotions, but continuing in the thank you after the storm has passed. Thank you for this insight and this person and this opportunity and this love. In spite of this and this and this, I thank you.

Long ago, I wrote a poem about the students to whom

I taught English as a Second Language. I was trying to find a way to honor who they were and I did it with the theme of conjugating the verb "to be" in both English and Spanish: "Yo soy (I am). Tu eres (You are)." If this sounds convoluted, just wait. It was a meditation on being. The poem closes with "Perhaps, *to be*, is saying *yes* to life. I am. You are."

Perhaps, to be, is saying yes to life. Perhaps, to be, is saying thank you to life. In the midst of it all. In spite of it all. Through it all. Thank you. Thank you. Thank you. I am. You are. I am grateful.

•INTENTION•

I choose to say *yes* to life.

> Thank you for the world so sweet.
> Thank you for the food we eat.
> Thank you for the birds that sing.
> Thank you God for everything. *Amen.*
> –CHILDHOOD PRAYER

"An attitude of gratitude is a never-ending prayer."
–UNKNOWN

"If the only prayer you say in your whole life is 'thank you,' that would suffice."
–MEISTER ECKHART

Harmony/Flexibility

KNITTING AND PURLING

W<small>HEN</small> I <small>WAS A LITTLE GIRL</small>, I lived with ten women in a three-story Victorian house in a small city in Texas. It was the middle of World War II and all the men were off to war.

My maternal grandmother, a widow who went out to work (unheard of in those days) and whose house it was, taught me much of what I know as a woman. One day she decided to teach me to knit. Knitting was no frivolous pastime. The soldiers (like my daddy and my uncles) at war needed mufflers. My aunt and my mother were both expecting babies. They needed blankets. It was time to go to work.

My fingers were long and thin. My nails were bitten off to the cuticles—I always nibbled them absentmindedly as I read in the window seat in the upstairs sitting room. Patiently my grandmother wrapped those fingers around fat, slick, shiny, colored needles with sharp points and showed me how to cast on stitches and cast them off, the yellow yarn snagging my fingers and then rolling under the sofa, the needles far too close to my near-sighted eyes. My grandmother explained about knitting and purling. Knit one row, purl one row. It's all opposites, and it makes a pattern. Knitting was when you held the needles and the yarn one way, looping it just so, and purling was when you held the needle and the yarn backwards and it made a different pattern. When you turned the length of knitting over, the knit side was the purl side and vice versa.

I struggled and perspired and concentrated. And I made a pattern. I was fascinated by this. Although I was never very domestic, I learned the rudiments of knitting.

Lately I have been reading about conflict resolution. Not either/or, black/white, bad/good, wrong/right, you lose/I win. But some way in which individuals, families, communities, nations, can use conflict resolution to —well, what else?—resolve conflicts. I've also been reading about how we can change our own interior conflicts by changing the way we think of them, by holding them in a new way, by looking at them from a different angle, by creating a new paradigm to encompass both points of view. Rather than either/or, we are to look for both/and. On a personal level, it's consciously choosing to see more than one solution to a problem, more than one way to end divisiveness. Choosing love and work, for example, instead of thinking in despair that if you have one, there's no room for the other. Or when, faced with the black-and-white thinking of 3:00 A.M. where you know that you'll never be happy again because of present despair, you can see and feel and know somehow, that having one emotion does not preclude the possibility of it all shifting and changing and becoming something else. That you can be an elderly woman and a successful artist. That you can be a young man and a good nurturer. That black/white assumptions, probably taught during earliest childhood and reinforced by an either/or society, can be changed to a harmonious weaving of both/and rather than either/or.

You can knit and you can purl. When you turn it over, the pattern is reversed. Both patterns are a part of the covering you are knitting, both a part of the gift you can give, whether to a child about to be born or a man needing warmth and comfort far from home. You can change the pattern any time you wish. You can knit one, purl two for example, and the pattern still exists, in reverse on the other side. You can drop a stitch or two, you can blacken the yellow wool with childlike hands, but the pattern still exists. In harmony and wholeness it exists.

Dear God,

Your harmony is everywhere. From a child's lesson with knitting to the opposites that exist in the world of adulthood. Teach me to recognize the hidden harmony within all things, so that I may see the harmony in the visible as well. In the name of peace, *Amen.*

"The hidden harmony is stronger than the visible."
–HERACLITUS

"Each small task of everyday life is part of the total harmony of the universe."
–ST. THERESA OF LISIEUX

Honesty

"I'VE PAID MY DUES"

A PERFECT STORY ON HONESTY, or the lack thereof, just fell into my lap. While traveling a few years ago in the West, I met a woman who owns a cement company, the sort of place where you would expect a rough-and-tumble, gritty, realistic, hunker-down, and do-your-work mentality.

My new acquaintance told me about hiring a flannel-shirted, blue-jeaned, earnest young man who swore by his church and his God that he would do an exceptional job for her company if she would only take a chance on him and hire him as the office manager. He had a wife and family.

So she hired the young man, let's call him Jake, and he did indeed prove exceptional. He came in early, at first, and stayed late, at first, and cleaned out the files and organized things on the computer. "He's the first man I've known who was a whiz with Windex," commented the owner, and she told how the dusty office began to sparkle and shine. Granted, he talked on the phone inordinately, questioned the hierarchy and rules of the company and watched zealously to see that no one except the owner and the president of the company got paid more than he did. In fact, he asked for raises and bonuses and vacation pay and sick leave pay as well as for frequent draws on his paycheck. He pouted and whined when he didn't get what he expected. The owner found that she spent an awful lot of time explaining just why she couldn't give Jake what he wanted.

But he was a good worker, and he did have a family, so the owner tolerated, at first, what she called his "Give-him-an-inch-and-he'll-take-a-mile" mentality.

One day Jake asked for another raise and refused to listen to any explanations from his boss. "I've paid my dues," he shouted. "I deserve more, a lot more."

In vain the owner tried to explain to him that he was at the top of the pay scale in terms of a small company. For the next few months, Jake repeated often to her, "But don't you see, I've paid my dues."

A no-nonsense woman, the owner realized that she had been babysitting this man while he nursed his grievances. She determined to let him go within a few months.

One day Jake came into her office. "I'm quitting," he said, "unless you can match my pay. I've got a new job, and they're paying me twice what you are."

"Congratulations," the owner said heartily. "Before you leave, let's sign these papers." They were for the money that Jake owed the company, a debt that had started small and escalated, due to his frequent "borrow-ings" whenever he got into a financial bind. After some unpleasantness, in which Jake reiterated that he had "paid his dues" and could now go where he would be appreci-ated, he signed the promissory note. The owner later found that before Jake left, he made hundreds of addi-tional dollars worth of personal charges on the company credit card, and paid himself an unauthorized bonus. All these transactions came to light only after he had left the company and a new office manager took over.

The owner could have taken Jake to court, could have tried to have him thrown into jail, could have called his new company and had him fired. Instead, she bided her time.

Three months later, Jake called. He hinted that he wanted his old job back. He had been let go in some reorganizational shake-up at the new company, or so he said. "They shafted me," he complained. And again, "I don't know why this happened to me. After all, I've paid my dues."

"But when are you going to pay me?" inquired my friend. There was silence on the other end of the phone and then the usual litany of excuses. The world was against him, and he didn't know why. Look how hard he'd tried. Would she give him a reference? No.

Such an obvious moral, but an apt one.

Truisms endure because they are true. "Honesty is the best policy." "What goes around comes around." "As ye sow, so shall ye reap."

The owner, who became a friend I've kept in contact with over the years, hired a new office manager, an efficient woman who cleared up the mess that Jake left. My friend's business prospers, year by year. Occasionally she gets a call from an employment agency, inquiring about Jake. "Can you give him a good reference? Is he a rehire?"

No, and again, no.

I'd love for this story to have a happy ending. Jake grows up. Jake gets a good job. Jake pays my friend back the money he borrowed from the company. Jake learns his lesson. It hasn't happened yet. Maybe someday, when Jake learns how the world works, it will. And then Jake will have paid his dues.

• I N T E N T I O N •

May I be honest with myself and others in all that I think, say, feel, and do.

"Each man takes care that his neighbor does not cheat him. But a day comes when he begins to care that he does not cheat his neighbor. Then all goes well. He has changed his market-cart into a chariot of the sun."

–RALPH WALDO EMERSON *(Worship)*

"We sow our thoughts, and we reap our actions. We sow our actions, and we reap our habits. We sow our habits, and we reap our characters. We sow our characters and we reap our destiny."

–ANONYMOUS

"When I do good, I feel good. When I do bad, I feel bad. And that's my religion."

–ABRAHAM LINCOLN

Hope

THE SOUL HAS ITS OWN AGENDA

WHEN MY SON MICHAEL was dying, there were two schools of thought to choose from, in order for the family and Michael to fight the disease. One school of thought was the doctors': "A germ is a germ. A virus is a virus. Here is the prognosis. We'll work with you to make the patient comfortable."

This was unacceptable to us. A bright and beautiful young man in his twenties, and this is it? A prognosis of doom. No. Fix it, please. Fix it now. We'll do anything.

The second attitude we encountered was that of the mind/body connection. I have no quarrel with that. To go a step farther, the mind/body/emotion connection. I have no quarrel with that. Surely a combination of physical, mental, and emotional therapies could address the whole person. Surely it would help. It did. For a while. Zealous proponents of the mind/body/emotional connection, however, were not kind to my son or our family. "You can think yourself well," they told him and us. "And if you do not think yourself well, if you continue to sicken and die, then it's your own fault. You must want to die, or else you would be in perfect health."

A little psychological knowledge is a dangerous thing. The conclusion to this rah-rah "you can do it" attitude was, for Michael, one of failure. Mind over matter could not get him through. Willpower could not get him through. Understanding and dealing with his inner conflicts could not get him through.

"You must have hope," people cried.

"There is no hope," said the doctor. "You are in denial. There is no hope."

Hope is not the same as denial. Denial implies that you do not recognize the reality before your eyes, even as you strive to change it with every fiber of your being.

And what of the spiritual? Some people, after all, go into remission with some diseases. Did we not pray hard enough? Did we not pray well enough? Did God not care? Why do some people live and some people die? And what does hope, that much maligned, much misunderstood word, have to do with a dying boy's fight for life?

We gave all our love to him. He gave all his love to us. Surely love heals? Let me have the hope that love heals.

Michael died loving. Michael died healing. Michael died in hope.

"The soul has its own agenda." These were the words that came to me in the last days of my son's life. These were the words that sustained me in my own journey through grief to resolution.

Here are the soul lessons. They have very little to do with the doctors' prognoses or the struggle of the mind and the emotions. They have very little to do with the body vehicle.

Michael wanted three things before he died. He asked that everyone in his family be healed. He asked to make a difference in the world. He asked to be surrounded and guided by unconditional love. I wrote about Michael's three wishes and the specific and miraculous and inevitable ways that those three wishes came true in an earlier book about Michael's life. Those three requests of his, made so fervently, so prayerfully, so hopefully, still guide my own life, long after Michael, in his physical form, has gone.

I still hope. I hope that when bad things happen to good people, which they do, that we will not lose hope. I hope that when tragedies wake with us and walk with us, and those we love go onward to a kinder, gentler place, that we can go onward too. I hope that we do not get caught in the literal, either/or syndrome, where only one course of action is possible, and when it fails, as indeed it might, that we do not chastise ourselves as failures, of the body, mind, emotions, or spirit. I hope above all, that we are kind to ourselves through all the soul lessons, through all our souls' agendas.

This story could just as easily be written about compassion or love or forgiveness or understanding. But I have chosen hope as a bright banner that unfurls onward and upward, no matter the earthly condition that lies under its flag of colors. I have chosen hope. And hope continues to fly before me and above me. I hope it always will.

•INTENTION•

I choose hope, again and yet again, through every condition, situation, or problem that I face in my life. I choose hope.

Dear God,
Help me to be hopeful through all the trials and tribulations of life. Help me to carry the bright banner of hope. May hope never die within me. Thank You. And so it is. *Amen.*

"Everything can be taken away from a man but one thing: the last of the human freedoms—to choose one's attitude in any given set of circumstances, to choose one's own way."

–VIKTOR FRANKL *(Man's Search for Meaning)*

Integrity

WHIPPED CREAM OVER WORMS

Hᴏᴡ ᴄᴀɴ ᴀ ʙᴏᴏᴋ ʙᴀsᴇᴅ on fifty positive qualities of the soul, and how to develop them, take space to write about the so-called negative emotions of life? We must make room for them, just as we make room for inner peace, balance, kindness, as well as hope, faith, and generosity. Because we are both dark and light, just as we are both inner and outer beings. So in order to embrace the soul of ourselves, we must look at all we are and all that we have felt, and all that we have experienced, and how we have come to the place where we are now.

Years ago, I coined a phrase in a book I wrote about my son's journey through AIDS. In it, I talked about the "whipped cream over worms" syndrome. That's when we cover up our grief, guilt, anger, fear, shame, resentment, bitterness, and any offshoots of our pain, by spreading a layer of sweetness, light, and positive thinking over the top. We ignore the pain, hoping it will just go away. We do not do the work of the soul. We pretend that we are all right. No, I have no quarrel with positive thinking. A spirit of optimism and a belief in the essential goodness of God, myself and other people has gotten me through some rough times. But I cannot pretend, when difficult times come, that I am all sweetness and light. I cannot do the work of the soul when politeness covers up my anger, when denial shoves my grief into my bones, when I refuse to look fear in the face, when undeserved and unwarranted threads of guilt weave a spider's web around my heart.

We are both human and divine. We are saint and sinner, courageous and cowardly, sometimes loving, sometimes hateful. When we pledge ourselves in prayer to become all that we can be, isn't it inevitable that the all that we can be contains both the attributes we long for and the recognition of the attributes we wish to transform?

I can say to you that I am far less angry than I used to be. But sometimes anger, deserved or undeserved, fuels me forward into great change. I can say to you that I have consciously and prayerfully given up old guilts that used to run my life. But there are still times when guilt knocks on the door of my heart and says, "Look at this. How can you do better?" Fear no longer haunts me on my daily rounds. But there are ancient echoes of it that rise up whenever new challenges occur.

Then why bother with spiritual development of any kind when in the end you are not all light but dark as well? Because a tree grows whether or not it is perfectly shaped. Because a child stumbles forward, lurching into new experiences, new competencies, a higher level of reasoning, past confusions of adolescence into the new challenges of adulthood. Because each piece of old baggage we transform—a fierce temper now mellower, peace of mind instead of all that guilt, courage in the face of every disaster we once feared—leaves us lighter, leaves us with more room for joy and creativity and love.

In a college psychology class twenty-five years ago, I heard a professor talk about the "eight stages of man." The task of later adulthood was to reassess your life. There were two choices available, according to the professor. These were integrity or disgust. I have never forgotten those words. How can we choose integrity unless and until we are integrated within ourselves as a whole person? Until and unless we have faced the worms under the whipped cream of the mask we wear in public? Unless and until we have done the work of the soul?

So how do we clear out the worms? An old mantra comes to me: Face, embrace, release, erase. Scoop aside the whipped cream over worms that has covered up your undesirable, disowned feelings. Do this privately in your meditation time, little by little. Face the unwanted negative emotion. Examine it, own it, feel it. Then objectify it, separate it from its moorings. It is not you. It is only a feeling about you. Then release the undesirable emotion, quality, or characteristic into the arms of the angels. Ask that the energy of it be transformed. Then drop the feeling from you insofar as you are able. (Don't worry, you'll get better with time.) Notice then how the emotion lessens, fades, dissipates.

So it's OK to have negative emotions. How can you not? It's what you do with them that matters. I choose integrity instead of disgust. It sure beats whipped cream over worms.

❧

•INTENTION•

I choose integrity in all that I think, feel, say, and do. And so it is.

"What is this darkness? What is its name? Call it: an aptitude for sensitivity. Call it: a rich sensitivity which will make you whole. Call it: your potential for vulnerability."

–MEISTER ECKHART

"To the extent that we honor all aspects of ourselves, we remove revulsion, self-hate, horror, and terror from our lives. As whole human beings we are the creatures of the greatest complexity on this planet. Respect for this complexity includes our insisting on acceptance of the inconsistent and incongruous."

–THEODORE RUBIN

"When I looked within myself, I found a zoo of lusts, a bedlam of ambitions, a nursery of fears, a harem of fondled hatred."

–C. S. LEWIS *(Surprised by Joy)*

Intuition

THE RADIANT NATURE OF THE MIND

ONCE WHEN A FRIEND and I were driving in the San Francisco Bay Area, she asked me what I did for fun. After going through the usual litany of friends, family, conversation, and books, I said in an extremely serious manner, "Of course what I really like to do is play with my mind." Laugh! She had to steer the car over to the curb and stop, she was laughing so hard. The image conjured up for her was that of a violin virtuoso, strumming on the brain, creating patterns and sounds and images. Well, she wasn't too far off. Thinking can be developed and practiced, just like any other skill. So can its partner, intuition.

What is intuition? Here is one explanation, tried, true, and tested by me in order to solve problems and to become more creative in every area of my life.

I think of intuition as a process in which knowledge comes in big chunks, all of a whole, in a nonlinear manner. Previously I learned to string together pieces of information one at a time, like stringing pearls on a necklace, or inputting strokes on a keyboard in a linear fashion, one stroke at a time, one word at a time. In intuition, knowledge comes all of a piece, clear and whole in itself, imprinted on the mind in a fraction of a second. Sometimes it comes in a visual diagrammatic form or in the form of a symbol. After the imprinting, the mind analyzes the information. If there is a need to translate this knowledge into normal human knowledge on a physical level, I believe that there is a "stepped-down process" to bring the information from inner knowledge into outer application. This is an integral part of the creative process.

Artists, writers, scientists, inventors often rely on these chunks of intuitive knowledge. They often come only after a person has saturated himself or herself with detailed outer knowledge on all the possible avenues that may lead to the solution of the problem, like making a mind map. First, all you may have is a clutter of detail without any economical pattern connecting them. Then, when least expected, and usually when you have given up on the problem, it is as if the sky has opened and the solution to the problem comes. It is received all at once, in its entirety, all details visible, yet now fitting together in an elegant order. Whether the culmination of years of search or one inspiring thought, it comes in an intuitive flash. The information is imprinted on the mind and is then decoded in our normal linear fashion. In a state of reverie, when the mind was not busying itself with anything in particular, the solution was received. The mind resonates with a higher level for a while and then absorbs the relevant information. This feels as though you have been given information out of the clear blue sky. It is a mystical process. Sometimes there is a feeling that time has come to a stop, in order for the information to be sent and received. That is the "aha," the "clunk" of knowing something new. It is like an elegant design, all of a whole, existing all at once, in more than one dimension.

Diane Mariechild, in *Open Mind*, refers to this wondrous process in this way: "We tend to identify thoughts and feelings with the mind, thinking they are the whole of the mind, when they are truly only the surface of the mind. Our minds are naturally clear, deep, and spacious, like the sky. Our thoughts and feelings are like clouds floating through that sky. And in the space between thoughts, the radiant nature of the mind shines through."

Developing intuition is just like developing any other muscle. Just as the athlete must train for years in order to become the best that he or she can be physically, so too those of us who love to play in the fields of the mind can exercise our skills in wondrous ways. Then we can continue, until the day we die, to let "the radiant nature of the mind" shine through.

• INTENTION •

I choose to explore this fascinating gift of mind that I have been given. I choose to develop my intuition and use my mind clearly and joyfully.

Dear Holy Spirit,
You have given me the gift of a sound mind in a sound body. Thank You for this gift, which I treasure. Help me to see clearly, to speak clearly, to communicate with everyone I meet with this gift of a clear mind. Help me to develop my intuition and strengthen my perceptions. Your radiant nature can then shine through me and from me to bless the world. *Amen.*

"We begin life with the world presenting itself to us as it is. Someone—our parents, teachers, analysts—hypnotizes us to 'see' the world and construe it in the 'right' way. These others label the world, attach names and give voices to the beings and events in it, so that thereafter, we cannot read the world in any other language or hear it saying other things to us. The task is to break the hypnotic spell, so that we become undeaf, unblind, and multilingual, thereby letting the world speak to us in new voices and write all its possible meaning in the new book of our existence. Be careful in your choice of hypnotists."

–SIDNEY JOURARD

"We spend most of our time and energy in a kind of horizontal thinking. We move along the surface of things, going from one quick base to another, often with a frenzy that wears us out. We collect data, things, people, ideas, 'profound experiences,' never penetrating any of them. . . . But there are other times. There are times when we stop. We sit still. We lose ourselves in a pile of leaves or its memory. We listen and breezes from a whole other world begin to whisper. Then we begin our 'going down.'"

– JAMES CARROLL

Joy

PLAY PARTY

IT WAS SUPPOSED TO BE A POOL PARTY, but it rained. Good friends, good food, good talk. There were twelve of us who showed up. I only knew two of them, my hostess and the friend who had brought me. Our ages ranged from twenty to eighty, and all points in between. We were male and female, married and single. What did we have in common?

We learned to play. We started with names of famous people pasted on our backs—a continuous, circulating guessing game as to who we were. I was Lucille Ball. No wonder I felt zany and jokey as the evening progressed. We told stories. We played games. We danced. We sang. We did a cakewalk with gag prizes. We played charades. I was great acting out *Up the Down Staircase.*

The seventy-nine-year-old woman playing charades with us said to us all, "It's just like when I was a girl, and we had play parties on Sunday night." Yes!

So then we reminisced about the way it used to be, growing up in rural areas, growing up in small-town America, growing up in a world where play parties on Sunday night were the norm, not the exception.

What struck me about this particular party was that there were no agendas and no egos. No one was there to advance their career or pick up someone. Since none of us smoked or drank (ah, the health-conscious '90s), there was no need for a designated driver, no fear of someone getting sloshed and out of control. Maybe it sounds boring to you. But to me, it spelled innocence reclaimed. Like sitting around a campfire with gentle people.

We've decided to get together about once a month and repeat the experience. Because we all need to learn to play again. To gather together in laughter and games. To generate joy from the inside out. And to share ourselves with friends.

What can I do to bring more joy into my life now?

•INTENTION•

I am determined to seek out and express joy in my life. I will look for joy in expected and unexpected places. And so it is.

"I'd rather learn from one bird how to sing than teach ten thousand stars how not to dance."

–EE CUMMINGS

"Decide to live joyfully, exultantly, gratefully, openly, and then miracles will begin to happen."

–ROBERT MULLER *(A Planet of Hope)*

"Joy is the infallible proof of the presence of God."

–TEILHARD DE CHARDIN *(A Planet of Hope)*

Kindness/Gentleness

CAMPFIRES OF KINDNESS

A FRIEND OF MINE, a woman who has lived in my hometown all of her life, saw a copy of a book about kindness on my coffee table. She leafed through it, and then looked at me in bewilderment. "I don't get it," she asked, puzzled. "This book tells me to do what I've been doing all my life." In vain I tried to explain to her the resurgence of the notion of kindness, to be acknowledged and practiced in large urban areas as well as in small hometowns. She shook her head in amazement. "You mean people pay money to be reminded to be kind?" she asked. She still didn't get it.

Much of my adult life is full of reminders. We recycle and remember what we once took for granted. We sort what works for us from the messages we were taught in childhood and we discard most of the learned behavior that caused us pain. But we hoard as well. We hoard those simple gems, those truisms, that lie underneath the surface of everyday life. What are manners exactly, if not the careful acts of thoughtfulness that we were taught? There used to be the concept of the gentleman and the gentlewoman. This may, for you, conjure up a rather

Victorian and fussy caricature of what it means to be a person. But for me, the concept of gentleness and its twin, kindness, are interwoven within the fabric of everyday life.

"Of course we are kind," exclaimed my friend. "How can we be anything else?" Really, we can't. The world's great religions teach us to "Do unto others as we would have others do unto us." And a simple book reminds us of the value of just that.

When I write these stories about my soul's way in the world, the tiny, unexpected acts of beauty revealed, as well as the huge life lessons that have come to me, I am not writing of anything new, rare, unexpected. Like you, I am groping my way to inner peace and serenity, step by step, sorting and discarding along the way. One of the qualities I think I'll keep is kindness. Purposeful, thoughtful, daily-practiced kindness. Maybe, like the proverbial ripple in the pond, each act of kindness will spread outward, until it is taken for granted all over the world. Then my friend, who always thinks in absolutes, can say "See! I told you so! Everybody is kind. It's a given." I hope she's right.

When I think of kindness and its twin, gentleness, I am struck by an image of campfires, lit in the darkness of lonely and vast spaces, sending up shoots of light, warming the hands and hearts of those huddled around the fires. Perhaps I am reminded of this because of a marvelous insight from Garrison Keillor, in which he says, "Even in a time of elephantine vanity and greed, one never has to look far to see the campfires of gentle people. Lacking any other purpose in life, it would be good enough to live for their sake."

Perhaps each of us, in our own way, could be a campfire of kindness for those around us. We could send up flares, sparks of light in the darkness, to say, "Here I am! Come and share my campfire. You don't have to be alone and cold and hurting. Here is simple human warmth."

And we could know, in that sharing, that we too, could run to other campfires of kindness when the need arose. Know that on many hills and in the valleys as well, exist campfires of kindness and gentle people. Close by. Right where we live.

•INTENTION•

I will use this proverb by William Penn as my intention of kindness this week: "If there is any kindness I can show, or any good thing I can do to any fellow being, let me do it now, and not deter or neglect it, as I shall not pass this way again."

"We cannot live only for ourselves. A thousand fibers connect us with our fellow men; and among those fibers, as sympathetic threads, our actions run as causes, and they come back to us as effects."

–HERMAN MELVILLE

"Kindness in words creates confidence. Kindness in thinking creates profoundness. Kindness in giving creates love."

–ENGLISH PROVERB

Learning/Knowledge

SOLVING PROBLEMS

Part of my ongoing Soulwork has been to learn how to handle my so-called negative emotions—the all-too-human responses of rage, guilt, shame, fear. I always leave grief out of the mix. There's been so much sorrow in my life, as there may have been in yours. Grief is not a mistake. It's an honorable response to the necessary losses of life. Now I'll bet you could add a few other emotions with which you struggle. Envy, resentment, jealousy, self-pity. We've all been there.

What do you do with these emotions? There's a current saying in psychology that says, "What you feel, you can heal." I have no trouble feeling. It's healing I'm interested in. I don't want my emotions, important as they are, to devastate my life. But I can no longer repress my feelings, put a cover over them, tell myself that they don't exist. My body won't let me.

A friend of mine is forever processing her emotions. That's OK, been there, done that, but then what? Can't lie on the couch all day, weeping at the turn your life has taken. Though you are allowed, even encouraged, to own and honor and feel your feelings. Just not for forever.

Of course there's prayer. Prayer's good. It lifts you out of yourself, unless your prayer is simply a begging bowl to be relieved of the emotion.

Sometimes my dreams serve to release the emotion I've been bottling up. Sort of like letting the dam break, but safely, while I'm asleep. You can discharge a lot of emotion that way. If you hold in your emotions, you run the very real risk of bottling up all the joyful creative parts of your life as well, becoming a repressed and rigid automaton.

I don't think you can solve a current problem by continuing in the emotion. You can acknowledge it, recognize, sniff around it like a dog sniffs a bone. You can douse the problem in tears or in righteous anger. You can express, express, express. And when it's still there, after all your work, what do you do?

A friend of mine, a wise and loving psychotherapist, gave me a set of tools that I can use when my feelings threaten to overwhelm me. She calls it "thinking through the feelings" or "how to think and feel at the same time." It's been a useful method for me. I'll share it with you.

She talks about emotions acting as signals. For example, the signal of anger means that I am not getting something I want or need at that moment. So I can stop and ask, in the middle of being mad, "What is it that I am not getting?" and "How can I get it in a healthy way?"

For me, this seems to short-circuit the emotion or at least calm it down a little. It shows me that I can use reason even in the midst of the emotion.

My friend goes on to say that the signal of being sad (as differentiated from overwhelming long-term grief, which is another story altogether) means that I feel that I am giving up something. So then I can ask myself "What am I giving up? Is it healthy to be giving it up?" And then, if the answer is "yes," I can begin to let it go. If the answer is "no," I can look at my choices. Either way, the sadness dissipates.

Moving right along, we come to the signal called scared. This signal alerts me that I need more information about the situation that is making me fearful or, in some cases, I need more protection. Sometimes I need both. So then I can ask myself, "What information and/or protection am I needing now?" And then, "How can I get it in a healthy way?" Then I can cease being so afraid.

The biggest area of emotional upheaval, for many of us a sort of continuing underground pattern, often unrecognized, is that of guilt. The signal of guilt is that of feeling that I have done something wrong. So then I can ask myself first, "Have I done something wrong?" If the answer is "yes," if I have in fact done something that wronged another person, I need to ask for forgiveness from that person and I also need to forgive myself. Sometimes only a brief apology is needed. When deeper issues are involved, you can refer back to the whole section on forgiveness and go through the seven steps to forgiveness in order to find a sensible and sensitive way of dealing with guilt (see Week Fifteen). But usually, according to my wise friend, when the signal of guilt rears its ugly head and I ask the question, "Have I done something wrong?" the answer is "no." This signals me that I am dealing with irrational guilt, which is nothing more than a sense of feeling wrong, usually based on someone else's opinion. Irrational guilt is insidious, often a lingering pervasive pattern. The answer to the irrational guilt is to recognize it for what it is (ah, relief!), let it go, and replace it with a feeling of self-worth.

There is much to be said for this method, which can, of course, be used to identify positive affirming emotions as well (I want more of those!). What this reasoning process has done for me is to give me tools to handle the ups and downs of everyday emotions without being at the mercy of them.

Here is another mastery technique. It's taking the bird's-eye view. You go up a level in your meditational work, where you can see the landscape of your problem in all its component parts. You fly above the problem and in doing so, you gain a new and clear and true perception.

You gain perspective. You gain distance. You get out of the wallow. Because a problem can never be changed at the level at which it was created. My first spiritual teacher, a woman minister, told me this, and the telling of it has been echoed back to me from various thinkers down the years. A problem can never be solved at the level at which it was created.

When you can see with new, true, and clear perception, you ask for help in changing the situation that has caused you so much pain. Changing the circumstances, if that is appropriate. Changing your mind or the minds of others. Doing it differently. Easing the pain emotionally. Walking away or seeing it through. It's all energy. And energy is infinitely changeable and infinitely transformable. You ask for wisdom, you ask for strength, you ask for courage, you ask for grace. And you release the problem into higher hands. You give it over. You let it go.

And always—always!—change occurs. "Everything changeth, God alone sufficeth," said St. Teresa of Avila.

And that's learning. That's knowledge. That's change. That's mastery.

•INTENTION•

I can learn new ways of handling my emotions and dealing with my problems. I let old ways and outworn concepts go, as I welcome positive change into my life through knowledge and mastery. And so it is.

"Learning is finding out what you already know. Doing is demonstrating that you know it. Teaching is reminding others they know it just as well as you. You are all learners, doers, teachers."

–RICHARD BACH *(Illusions)*

"You can't solve a problem on the same level that it was created. You have to rise above it to the next level."

–ALBERT EINSTEIN

Love

LOVE AND EXPECTATIONS

ONCE UPON A TIME, long, long ago, my then-husband and I went to marriage counseling. The pastoral counselor told us, I remember this with great vividness and clarity, "If you want more love, be more loving." The marriage did not survive the counseling. The advice did.

How do you encapsulate love, its meaning and application, into a page or two of Soulwork principles? Are we talking here about love between men and women, love for your children, family, friends, work, country, the world? Are we talking here about loving God? Are we talking about loving ourselves more and more, being kinder and gentler with ourselves each passing year? Yes, yes, and again yes to all of the above.

I wrote a poem once that had to do with what I perceived continuing, flowing, ever-expanding love to be. It said in part: "I cannot check my love in little contracts. The more I love, the more I give to love."

I have observed, though, that love usually does imply contracts between people, legal or implied, spoken or unspoken, assumed and expected.

As I grow older and hopefully wiser, and certainly, I

pray with all my heart, become a more loving human being, I find it much easier to love when someone else's expectations don't overshadow all that I want and choose to give in love. And I do better with loving without my own expectation of being loved in return, without the expectation that if I am more loving, someone will love me back, and I'll get what I've been searching for.

When I am loving in my thoughts, and loving in my work, and loving to other people, I feel it as a soft, gentle candle of energy that flows from my heart to yours. Not the passionate raptures and yearnings of yesteryear. But something steady, something you can count on.

There is a saying called "Namaste." You may have heard it. When two people meet, you clasp your hands together in prayer position, nod your head to that person, and say, "Namaste." It means, "I behold the Divinity in you." You acknowledge the love within them, and you offer salutation in return. One of my teachers called it "the God salutation." Perhaps this is what Mother Teresa is talking about when she talks about the Christ within each individual. Loving that spark within.

"If you want more love, be more loving." Be more loving even if you don't want, need, or expect more love in return. Be more loving just because of the spark of God-love within you. Namaste. I behold the love and the Divinity within you.

❧

"There isn't any secret formula or method. You learn love by loving—by paying attention and doing what one thereby discovers has to be done."

–ALDOUS HUXLEY

"We ourselves feel that what we are doing is just a drop in the ocean. But if that drop was not in the ocean, I think the ocean would be less because of the missing drop. I do not agree with the big way of doing things. To us what matters is the individual. To get to love the person we must come in close contact with him. . . . I believe in person to person; every person is Christ for me . . . that person is the one person in the world at that moment."

–MOTHER TERESA

"When you break your craving for love into its component parts, you can address it. Instead of focusing on the love you are not finding, shift to the experience you are having with love, with connection, with recognizing your life force taken up and shared. As you do this, you open a doorway to deeper love, and further connection."

–ELLEN MEREDITH *(Listening In: Dialogues with the Wiser Self)*

Nobility

NOBILITY AND WORK

A WOMAN IS CLEANING MY HOUSE TODAY. She is the student of an old friend of mine, who, like me, has taught English as a Second Language to adults for years. She still teaches, while now I write. She suggested one of her students, Mary, who needed work. I needed her.

There is nothing unusual in having help around the house, having some other woman come in and scour and polish and mop and put everything in order. Especially when one works full-time. But for me, it is unusual. There's that little niggling finger of guilt. I've done my own housework for years. I was raised to clean up my own space. Yes, but now my back hurts when I mop and I don't have the agility to reach the windows, either inside or out, and besides, I've got my own work to do. So I'm hiring someone else to clean up my space.

I pretty much work alongside her, my halting Spanish instructing, while I sort files and rearrange closets. There's plenty for both of us to do. Backbreaking work for both of us, for her more than me.

When I taught English as a Second Language, one of my students told me once, "Todo trabajo es noble" (all work is noble). She was a middle-aged, stocky, plain-faced woman who worked as a domestic. She was contributing to a discussion that had started in the classroom when a beautiful young woman, the daughter of a diplomatic family that had fled Cuba, was lamenting the loss of her schooling and her bright career. We often used these free-wheeling discussions to practice not only talking in English but thinking in English as well. I had no doubt that this young woman, willing to start over in a strange land, willing to learn English at night, possessed of beauty and brains and drive, would rise to the highest position of which she was capable. She had success written all over her. But the words of the plain older woman were the ones that stuck in my mind: "Todo trabajo es noble."

I asked her what her favorite job was. "I like to wash the windows," she said. "Why?" I asked her. "Because then the sun, she can shine into," she answered in her halting English. I did not correct her grammar.

"Because then the sun, she can shine into." Isn't that what I attempt, years later, with every passage I write? With every Soulwork lesson that I learn? When you clear away everything that is heavy, dark, grimy, cobwebby, ugly, "then the sun can shine into."

Mary and I work side by side, in amiable companionship. I get to practice my Spanish and put order into my life. She is raising three children. Her husband works and goes to school at night to study computers. They are on their way. She washes the windows in my office. They sparkle and gleam. The sun shines through onto my polished, newly organized desk.

"Mucho trabajo," I say to her (much work). "Si," she answers, "Poco a poco, toda limpia." (Little by little, everything gets clean.)

Sooner or later, little by little, everything gets clean and clear and shining and bright. You just keep on working at it. Because "Todo trabajo es noble."

"But is work something that we have a right to escape? And can we escape it with impunity? We are probably the first entire people ever to think so. All the ancient wisdom that has come down to us counsels otherwise. It tells us that work is necessary to us, as much a part of our condition as mortality; that good work is our salvation and our joy; that shoddy or dishonest or self-serving work is our curse and our doom. We have tried to escape the sweat and sorrow promised in Genesis—only to find that, in order to do so, we must forswear love and excellence, health and joy."

–WENDELL BERRY *(The Unsettling of America)*

"Work is love made visible. "
— KAHLIL GIBRAN *(The Prophet)*

How do I feel about my work?
Is my work love made visible? If not, what can I do to
express love in my work? What can I do to honor my tasks?
What can I do to make my work a noble endeavor?

Optimism/Enthusiasm

FIRST DAY OF SCHOOL

I'VE ALWAYS WONDERED why New Year's Day, with its resolutions, its goals, its blank pages, its starting over, comes in January, at the darkest and coldest part of the year. For me, early September, the first day of school, is always and forever my New Year's beginning. Because I was married to a school principal for many years, and taught school myself, and had four sons who attended various neighborhood schools, everything in our household revolved around that new beginning each year. It's been a lot of years. I seldom talk about that part of my life, it seems so far away. Now my children have children to get ready for school.

There's an excitement in the air, although in this part of the country, it still feels like summer. They call it Indian summer here, that time when the heat has not yet left, and yet the leaves are beginning to turn golden and red and rust and brown, and the mornings are crisp. New sneakers and new jeans and new haircuts, new lunchboxes labeled with each child's name. New books. New studies. New friends. New teachers. New lessons. New opportunities. New. Everything new. Everything possible.

It's been hard for me to be an optimist lately. I've been dragging my body and my responsibilities around like a millstone around my neck. I've been grumbling at chores and deadlines, feeling out of sorts. Will the heat ever leave? Will this summer ever end? Will my life ever change?

But today the yellow school buses stopped on each corner. And the crossing guards put on their belts and took their signs and oh so importantly, allowed that stream of rowdy, excited youngsters to cross in front of the stopped cars. The young mothers walked their children to school in my neighborhood, sometimes with a stroller or toddler in tow, and walked their children home again at three. There's a school for special kids three blocks away. There's the high school a half-mile away. There's the university only a block and a half away. So wherever I turn my car, I see hundreds of people, of varying ages, all—all!—faced with new beginnings. When I go to the library in the late afternoon, serious students are already there, with the smell of old books and new notebooks spread out around them. When I go to the office supply store, there are excited lines of children with their arms full of supplies, while their mothers pour over the official lists of what they need. At lunchtime the cafes and the walkways and the benches on campus are filled with teachers and college students. This weekend, I'll be able to hear the cheers of the crowd from the stadium as the first college football game starts. You won't be able to get through the streets around the college. You'll only be able to hear the cheers. It almost makes me wish, just for a moment, that I was again a part of their world.

But then common sense reasserts itself. I have no wish to be confined in classrooms. What I do wish for is that boundless optimism that the new school year brings. That sense of unlimited possibility, that sense that this year will be good, this year will be better, this year will be filled with joy and learning both at the same time.

So I stand in line at the office supply store with the children and their mothers. I don't mind that the store is crowded and noisy and I have to wait. I hold new pencils and new notebooks in my hand. I've bought colored filecards and colored folders. I'm ready for my new year. And I am eager, excited, enthusiastic, energetic. I am full to the brim. Optimistic. Ready to begin again.

Dear God,

Help me to begin again with joy, cheerfulness, optimism, and enthusiasm in my heart and in my endeavors. Thank You. And so it is. *Amen.*

"It is energy—the central element of which is will—that produces the miracle that is enthusiasm in all ages. Everywhere it is what is called force of character and the sustaining power of all great action."

–SAMUEL SMILE

"Cheerfulness in most cheerful people is the rich and satisfying result of strenuous discipline."

–EDWIN PERCY WHIPPLE

Patience

NOTHING IS EVER WASTED

THE OTHER DAY I ran across a saying about creativity by M. C. Richards that expresses both patience and practice. It's just this: "All the arts we practice are apprenticeship. The big art is our life."

Have you ever noticed that some expressions, some lines of words stitched together, leap into your heart and burrow there? You cannot dislodge them. They resonate within you, and days, weeks, months, years later, you are still walking around, muttering lines that haunt you. Because I am a writer, I am sensitive to the power and persistence of words, but I believe that I am not alone in this. We carry words within us like signposts to mark the passages of our lives.

There were decades of my life where the learning was difficult, and the living wasn't easy. During one such time, in my forties, when a long, long marriage was crumbling despite heroic intentions, I began to write a poem. I thought it was meant to be an outpouring of love's exhaustion and bitter defeat. In fact, one line read, "Say you tried. Rest on your wrecked devices."

But like so many other events in my life, bitterness

could not be sustained. Although I was mourning the death of a love, my spirit emerged in an anthem at the end:

Done. Owned by no one. Alone.
Flying free, uncaged,
You have come of age.
Nothing is ever wasted, merely postponed.

Funny how life imitates art. Eleven years later, the words sing through me. Echoing my present truth. A quiet anthem.

Nothing is wasted. Not words, not deeds, not heartbreak, not tragedy. Not ever wasted, years lived fully. Not ever wasted, love's long learning.

And now, dare I say it? Older, wiser, better, nothing, nothing, nothing, is postponed.

What does the word "patience" mean to you?
Is patience its own reward? Are there signposts of patience
along the way that indicate how far you have come?

•INTENTION•

May the words of my mouth and the meditations of my heart resonate with the truth of my quiet anthem of patience—all that is mine will come to me, and nothing is postponed.

"It does not astonish or make us angry that it takes a whole year to bring into the house three great white peonies and two pale blue irises. It seems altogether right and appropriate that these glories are earned with long patience and faith . . . and also that it is altogether right and appropriate that they cannot last. Yet in our human relations we are outraged when the supreme moments, the moments of flowering, must be waited for . . . and then cannot last. We reach a summit, and then have to go down again."

–MAY SARTON

"If I could only remember that the days were not bricks to be laid row on row, to be built into a solid house, where one might dwell in safety and peace, but only food for the fires of the heart."

–EDMUND WILSON

Peace

WHO NEEDS PEACE?

ONCE I WAS AT A BUSINESS MEETING with a new publisher, her associate, and the publicist she had hired to launch a book I had written. The publicist, a dynamic, bright, and forceful woman, was trying to find a way to make me stand out from the crowd. "Are you an investigative reporter?" she asked eagerly. "No, I'm more of a teacher, really." She made a face. Too dull for words. "Are you an innovator, a trailblazer, tops in your field?" "Well, really, I just write books about the heart and the soul and the ways that people can get through life with an inner compass." I had lost her. She tried once again. "Are you an expert on the meaning of life? And if so, what is it?" I answered her unhesitatingly. "I'm no expert. I'm still learning, as are the people I interview. But we're all searching for the same thing." "What, for heaven's sake?" "Inner peace, of course," I replied. "In fact, that's the next book I want to write. A book on inner peace."

She made a face. "I can't sell inner peace," she protested. "It's not hot. It's not trendy. It's not . . ." her voice trailed off. "It's not anything."

Ah, but yes it is. I can, of course, continue her explanation of what it is not. It is not passive. It is not static. It is not some state of beautification where we are unresponding, uninvolved with the rest of the world.

Inner peace is active. Inner peace is an ever-changing dynamic of strength, serenity, wisdom, and love. It is a fullness within, not an emptiness. It is the inner fortitude with which we approach the world. It is a steady candle within, that does not waver or blow out when hard times come. Inner peace is inner equilibrium. It is balance.

Don't you think everyone on the planet would really desire, in their heart of hearts, to experience inner peace? Don't you think that we're all looking for that blessed sanctuary of strength within? A place where we are not swayed by fame or fortune or the lack of either, a place where steadiness blossoms and love heals? Where giving and receiving are the same? A place of access to the Divine?

I yearn for inner peace. It tiptoes in, more and more, as I make room for it. As I welcome it. As I build on it.

Who needs peace? Everyone. Who wants peace? Everyone. Who can experience peace? Everyone.

Begin now.

Deep peace of the Running Wave to you.
Deep peace of the Flowing Air to you.
Deep peace of the Quiet Earth to you.
Deep peace of the Shining Stars to you.
Deep peace of the Son of Peace to you.
—CELTIC BENEDICTION

"There is no way to peace. Peace is the way."
—A. J. MUSTE

Dear Peaceful Power,
I yearn for peace in every part of my being, in every avenue of my life. I ask for Your peace and power to accompany me throughout each day. Let me be peace on earth. I am willing to begin now to allow more and more peace into my life. With Your help, *Amen.*

Perseverance

SAILING AND STUMBLING AND
ALL POINTS IN-BETWEEN

O H, THE THINGS I can tell you about perseverance! Listen well, my children and you shall hear. There's not a soul I know in this day and age on this planet who hasn't had to go through the long, slow, agonizing, difficult lessons of perseverance. We've come through.

I was reminded of this when a woman named Ann asked her friends for help in understanding just what had happened or was going to happen to her seminar business. Her skills helped people all over the country to plan their lives for the next twenty years. Yet she was hitting stone walls in her own life whenever she tried to expand and go forward.

"I'm the type of person who doesn't let obstacles get in my way," she explained to this group of friends. "I'll ram my way through glass ceilings and stone walls. But now, it isn't working. I'm frustrated and tired."

We all had stories of our own to match hers and stories of the ways that we had gotten through. But none of the analogies seemed to help. Finally another woman suggested that Ann close her eyes and tell us what she saw when she usually thought of herself and her business. She did and said she saw a powerful speedboat, slicing through the water until it ran out of water and room. Until it overturned.

The same woman then suggested, "What I see that you need now, is to think of yourself as a sailboat instead of a speedboat, to tack and turn and sail in a leisurely way across the water, to go with the wind and the tides instead of only on your own steam. To harness the power of the wind instead of burning up your motor. And to rest on the deep blue swells of the sea, now and then, and watch the clouds go by. And then let the sailboat find its way."

This was powerful advice for her. It struck a chord with me too. So often we work in a linear fashion, going from one straight line to the next, whether we are moving horizontally or vertically. The only way is straight ahead. The only way is up. I remember hearing a quaint saying years ago and applying it to my own life: "Life is hard by the yard. But inch by inch, it's a cinch." It helped me keep my nose to the grindstone and my vision focused straight ahead. It worked for me then. But I'm leery of that particular aphorism now. For I have discovered that perseverance can operate in a zigzag fashion, in a circular fashion, in a widening and rounding-out fashion as well as by my charging straight ahead, butting my head against steel doors and becoming bloody and dazed in the process.

When we look back on our lives, at how far we've come, aren't the twistings and the turnings of the road and perhaps exploring new roads altogether, a part of the fascinating journey of life?

I used to be *The Little Engine that Could.* You remember that children's story, don't you? I'll never forget it. Chugging uphill or downhill, laboring with all its might and all its engines running. "I think I can. I think I can. I know I can. I know I can." And then, of course, he could and did get to his destination.

Ursula LeGuin has given us a famous quotation about that very process. In *The Left Hand of Darkness* she says: "It is good to have an end to journey toward; but it is the journey that matters, in the end."

In Soulwork, as in life, it is the journey itself that matters. Not *how* you persevere but *that* you persevere. And we will get there, we will. I have no doubt. But the way changes. Perhaps by floating on a sailboat and watching clouds, rather than taking the shortest distance between two speeding points, engines roaring all the way. I think I'll try it.

❧

Are there new ways for me to reach my goals?
Am I willing to explore alternate avenues?
Am I willing to do things differently?

• INTENTION •

This week I will persevere in gentleness and grace.

"I don't want to get to the end of my life and find that I lived just the length of it. I want to have lived the width of it as well."

–DIANE ACKERMAN

"To reach the port of Heaven, we must sail sometimes with the wind, sometimes against it, but we must sail, and not drift, nor lie at anchor."

–OLIVER WENDELL HOLMES

"By your stumbling, the world is perfected."

–SRI AUROBINDO

Power

RESULTS FOLLOW AFTER

"GREAT POWER WILL BE GIVEN only where great power is generated." These startling words come from one of my most-loved books, a dog-eared first edition I have carried with me all over the country for many years.

Letters of the Scattered Brotherhood is not some esoteric text but a collection of anonymous essays by Anglican clergy, written as spiritual messages to give hope and help to those Londoners going through the Blitz during World War II. These messages have survived because, as the passages were read and contemplated, they formed not only canticles of courage but a clear direction for a strong interior life. "When you live with the great forces that beat your heart, and work through the involuntary activities of the body, you are given assurance because of your rejection of weakening terrors, and you find immediate response in health and wisdom in your daily life. More and more will you realize the relief throughout your nervous system, and the organization of your body will collaborate and assist you in generating the spirit of victory, of 'dominion over all your earth-consciousness.'"

These are letters of genuine spiritual experience. They

speak to the reader of today as a text of overcoming fear and living with a serene inner courage. They also speak of power.

The only true power is inner power.

How is true power generated? In daily life, by living what you are, in private times, questioning, searching, seeking, through prayer and contemplation, building interior muscles of faith and wisdom. As true power is generated, you cannot be false. If you are working on the soul quality of peaceful and dynamic power, it is not enough to wish, want, desire, ask for that soul quality. It is a beginning only.

Rather, it is in asking these questions: How can I be more powerful in my loving? How can I be more powerful in my wisdom? How can I be more powerful in my compassion? How can I be more powerful in my faith? How can I be more powerful to others and to myself? Where is the opportunity to be more powerful? Sweep away all your previous ideas of what power is and is not, because the word itself is so often misused, misunderstood, and misapplied. Just ask the questions and listen for the answers. Ask to be guided to your own genuine and beneficent power.

When you work with the thought of value, of service, of throwing your love and work powerfully outward into the world, it will find its own true place. And that is interior power. You can learn the skills, the skills of loving, the skills needed for your work, the skills of awareness in each moment. You can learn the niceties and the dynamics of interacting with the world. But true power, like everything else of value in life, is an inside job.

Soulwork is not about power over. Soulwork is about true inner power developed through the accessing of the Divine within and the spiritual practice of bringing the Divine within to the outer work of the world. It is a lifelong task. True power, to me, feels quiet and sweet and strong, a flowing creativity that changes as I change. True power, to me, feels like concentrated light, like consecrated light. True power, to me, feels like inner mastery and outer balance. I've barely begun to open the door to that inner power. But it is opening to me in prayer. I ask, again and again I ask, that it continue. *Letters of the Scattered Brotherhood* tells me: "If you ask for this it will come like the waters of life from outer and inner darkness. It is clean and still and far and wide and high and deep: it is glorious beyond the feeling of rejoicing."

It goes on to say: "Wake then, little, perturbed, anxious, weary, frightened children, and stand released in this holy stillness; then will the picture be fulfilled. Results follow after. Be in a place that brings results."

Results follow after. We practice our Soulwork, our inner studies, and our outer work in the world. We are translators, bridging the interior to the exterior. We walk in balance on that bridge. We become our own true power. Results follow after.

•INTENTION•

I am guided by God in my discovery of my own true inner power. As I pray, meditate, ask, listen, contemplate, and reflect, my inner power blossoms into light. I am guided by God in the wise and loving use of my inner power, and I generate good and more good, an ever-widening circle of good. And so it is.

"I do not ask of God that He should change anything in events themselves, but that He should change me in regard to things, so that I might have the power to create my own universe, to govern my dreams, instead of enduring them."

–GERARD DE NERVAL

Receiving

FAMILY POSSESSIONS

MY MOTHER MOVED FIVE TIMES in one year, from home to assisted living community, from floors of activity to levels of increasing care, and finally into a skilled nursing floor at another health center, her final move in this lifetime.

One of my sisters helped me move her. Again and again we moved her.

For the first move, my mother and I took a week of ten-hour days to sort, catalog, and give to each family member, from the oldest son-in-law to the newest great-granddaughter, specific treasured mementos of my mother's life. Perhaps one sister would have preferred the antique desk instead of the antique buffet, or great-grandmother's plates instead of the wicker porch chairs. No matter. Nary a cross word was spoken. I thought it was remarkable.

Each time my mother declined in health, in an ever-downward, ever-decreasing spiral of movement, my sister and I moved her again. By the last move, we had had it. We had already given to Goodwill and the woman's shelter and the community church. We had given and given

and given away, but still my mother's possessions col-
lected. Both family treasures and dusty silk flower
arrangements. We kept on finding more and more with
every box we moved from place to place.

"You take this!"

"No, you take it."

"I don't want it. I've got too much stuff already."

"Well, I don't have room."

"Who can we give it to?"

"Maybe this grandchild would like the couch."

"Maybe this granddaughter will take these lamps."

"You've got to store all the rest. Mother still wants
these things, just in case."

"Just in case?"

"She thinks she may get better, and she thinks that
someday, she may want all these things."

"Oh no! Just take this."

"I'm already storing stuff from the last move. You take
this."

"No, you take it!"

We rocked in laughter and fatigue as we tried to give
away my mother's possessions.

It was a sweltering day. I was going to the car with
arms full of clothes I doubted my mother would ever
wear again, when my sister thrust two hanging baskets of
flowers into the back seat of my car. They had graced

either side of my mother's doorway for years, at the home she loved so much, the one with the hand-painted ducks that said "Welcome" on the front door.

I am not good with plants or flowers. I have the best intentions, but I forget to water them. I don't even talk to them.

"No! You take them!" I said.

"I don't want them. You take them!"

I took them. I set the hanging baskets in an untidy heap on my terrace, on a white wrought-iron table that I had inherited from an earlier move of my mother's, and promptly forgot about them.

The summer lengthened and drooped with drought and heat.

Everything living just about died. At ten o'clock each night, it was still in the high nineties. Too hot to walk. Too hot to do anything except sit on the terrace and watch the stars.

One night my gaze fell on a corner of the terrace. There were flowers growing there. Pushing up from inside the flagstones of the terrace, pink and purple flowers. Yards away from the unexpected blooms, the hanging baskets sat, dried, dusty, dead. How had the flowers gotten there? But there they were. All summer long they bloomed. Direct sunlight, no water. Even the lawn care man couldn't uproot them, the time or two he tackled the weeds around the terrace steps. Maybe the squirrels, who had eaten my other plants, had scattered the seeds. Or maybe it was the wind. Nevertheless.

I walk through my spacious house, more crowded now than I would ever choose, crowded with the cherished, much-used possessions of the generations of women from which I spring. I give away a table, a set of glasses, some sheets and towels. I give away pictures. I give away clothes. I give away piles of books.

My mother is very ill. This is the truth of her situation for almost four years. I pick up a needlepoint pillow she made for me. I hug it to my chest. I sleep in my grand-mother's brass bed, the one her grandmother brought from Tennessee to Texas in a covered wagon. I read in bed by the light of the floor lamp that I read from as a child. I sleep under the crocheted afghan that once graced my mother's bed.

My mother's flowers bloom on.

How do I really feel about receiving? Am I able to receive as well as give? When receiving means the impending death or destruction in someone else's life, how can I learn to accept and receive the messages inherent in life's changes? Can I learn to be at peace about receiving?

· I N T E N T I O N ·

This week I will look beyond the gifts given and the gifts received to the true messages of life given and received. This week I will cherish the gifts I have been given and the family possessions that speak to me of loving memories.

O God,

I come to You with outstretched heart and hands, to receive the gifts that You have for me. Sometimes receiving is painful and my heart fills up with grief. Yet I know that there is a plan and a purpose in these gifts given and received, just as there is a plan and a purpose within each new challenge in a loved one's life. Gratefully I give out of my bounty. Gratefully I receive from all the seasons of life. And so it is. *Amen.*

"It is better to give *and* receive."

–BERNARD GUNTHER

"I am not worried about possessions anymore, but each one of them tells a story. I notice the objects, rugs, furniture, and photographs and am reminded of the lessons that needed to be learned at that time. I consciously remember, so that I don't forget again. It is an art—to recollect an experience in past time, knowing that in reality there is no such thing, and to bring the experience into present time is a useful form. The key is relatively simple, and that is that we are continuously being given experiences, out of which we can learn. Once understood, we do not need the experience anymore. Perhaps the greatest teacher and lesson of all is life itself."

–RESHAD FEILD *(The Invisible Way)*

Resilience

CHANGING FORM

In *Soulwork* I wrote about some of the changes in my life that had forced me to look deeply within my inner self. These included leaving my home in Texas and starting over in Los Angeles, the illness and death of my beloved son Michael, starting my own business, working in the AIDS crisis for seven years, the dissolution of my business and my life goals in Los Angeles, and the relocation back to my roots for healing, reflection, and renewal. These were not the only changes, by far, that occurred. A lifetime of lessons about illness, caregiving, death, loss, and renewal have accompanied me through much of my life.

The difference in me now is that where once I resisted these changes, these losses, with every bit of will and force I could muster, now I see my life as more of a pattern, with both its losses and its triumphs woven into an intricate and interesting and ever-changing weave. In other words, I've learned resilience.

There have always been wonderful teachers and counselors along the way that have helped me through life's difficult moments. One of these was a priest and therapist who helped guide me through the grief and challenges I encountered after the death of my son, and other deaths I was facing as well. I would go to him for guidance and comfort as I sorted out the challenges in my life. When my business collapsed, I thought I would collapse as well. That's when my friend and counselor told me about form.

"You are still here," he told me, "with all your will and all your spirit and all your love. Who you are can never be taken away from you. Only the form of your life is changing. Your mission in the world, the people you associate with, the possessions, the location, the opportunities, may change. You are still here. Everything else may go. You are still here."

Only the form changes. In an instant I could see that what looked like impending bankruptcy and the death of all my dreams was, in reality, simply the dissolving of an old form so that a new form could emerge.

My friend spoke of resilience, he spoke of courage, he spoke of clarity. "You can walk through this trial by fire," he told me. "You have eyes to see clearly, you have ears to hear clearly. Your fear and anger and sorrow are natural responses to these changes in your life. But you will not drown in your emotions. You have come too far for that. Just remember, everything in life changes form. You are entering a new season of your life."

His words helped me through a difficult, life-altering

time. His words help me now. I hope they will help you.

Only the form changes. Relationships may fail, people may die, businesses may fold, locations may shift, possessions may fall away. We move on. We keep moving on. Only the form changes. We continue.

Dear God,

Thank You for teaching me about changing form. Thank You for the seasons of my life and the seasons of my soul. I await change with anticipation, not trepidation. I welcome positive change and the good it brings to me now. With Your loving help and in Your loving name, *Amen.*

"You must understand the whole of life, not just one little part of it. That is why you must read, that is why you must look at the skies, that is why you must sing, and dance, and write poems, and suffer, and understand, for all that is life."

–J. KRISHNAMURTI *(Think on These Things)*

"There is a time for expanding and a time for contraction; one provokes the other and the other calls for the return of the first. . . . Never are we nearer the Light than when darkness is deepest."

–SWAMI VIVEKANANDA

"A change is never a finished product. It is a shift in the way you move through life. It is an alteration of attitudes, beliefs, feelings that affect your choices. It is a movement in a particular direction, which takes your life into new territory and new dreams, each presenting their own new challenges to you. Change is a turning wheel which carries you into new realms one inch at a time."

–ELLEN MEREDITH *(Listening In:*
Dialogues with the Wiser Self)

" 'Why,' a seventy-six-year-old woman was asked, 'are you seeking therapy at your age?' Reflecting both her losses and her hopes, she answered, 'Doctor, all I've got left is my future.'"

–JUDITH VIORST *(Necessary Losses)*

Respectfulness

TOO MUCH SELF-ESTEEM

I AM VERY FORTUNATE in that I am a part of a group of women who meet regularly for problem solving, spiritual insight, friendship, and support. We respect one another's boundaries even as we laugh and cry and pray together, even as we cut to the heart of the matter when a problem is presented for discussion. The other day, my friend Carol said, half-laughing and half-crying, "The last man I was with told me that I had too much self-esteem. And then he left."

Carol is a single mother in her forties. She has a two-year-old toddler she is raising alone, while she works as a therapist with gang members in a multiracial setting, commutes back and forth to a private practice in psychotherapy, and juggles babysitters and the terrible two's along with overdue bills, all the while maintaining a close relationship with her mother, sister, and her good friends. She is deeply spiritual and has also worked with troubled teenagers in a church setting. She plans to extend her practice into working with nursing homes and the elderly.

She is, in other words, a beautiful, compassionate, wise, loving, hardworking, healthy, spiritual, multidimensional woman. And she would like to have a loving, committed relationship with a man. Yet the stronger she gets, or so it seems to her, the less likely she is to find a man of her caliber. She is forlorn and angry about the message she received from her last male friend.

"You cannot be less in order for someone else to be more," we tell her in unison. "You cannot be passive when you are powerful, weak when you are strong. You cannot!" And we tell her, loudly and clearly and in chorus, "There is no such thing as too much self-esteem."

How could there be? As we grow mentally, emotionally, and spiritually, we become stronger and surer and wiser. We do not eradicate the ego. The ego is a part of us, a friend who helps us in our daily tasks. Neither do we become less in our womanliness or maleness, in our convictions or our characters. We become both deeper and higher. We stretch toward God while we work diligently on earth. We embrace more of what we are and more of what we can be. But we do not become less. We do not diminish ourselves in order to please another person. I think it all boils down to an attitude of respectfulness to one another. Male to female, and female to male. Mother to child, and friend to friend. To treat not only others with respect, courtesy, and lack of manipulation but to treat ourselves with the same respectfulness. My friend Carol is helping her young son to become a good man. To respect others. To respect himself. She does this by respecting herself and the people with whom she comes into contact. You can see it in her gaze. You can hear it in her voice.

A Zen proverb states: "Sit, walk, or run, but don't wobble." We share this with one other, acknowledging how far we have come on our own individual, clear paths. Carol does not wobble. She has too much self-esteem for that.

Is there anyone in your life who tries to limit you, define you, squelch you, attempt to make you less than you are? If so, what can you do to change the situation?

• A F F I R M A T I O N •

I welcome and give thanks for continuing and ever-increasing self-esteem. I honor who I am.

"We must not allow other people's limited perceptions to define us."

–VIRGINIA SATIR

"Nobody can make you feel inferior without your consent."

–ELEANOR ROOSEVELT

Responsibility

DO YOU MELT?

MY MATERNAL GRANDMOTHER had a saying to describe people who folded into a heap whenever life got difficult or whenever they were called upon to go beyond their accustomed limits to care for others. She called them "Sugar Christians."

"They just melt at the first drop of rain from the sky," she told me. "They may say sweet and pious things, but they just melt into a heap of sugar on the sidewalk."

Although I have pledged to give up my judgments of others whenever possible, my grandmother's pithy saying echoes in my ears—especially when times get tough, and I or someone I love needs help. This has happened to me more than once, and for long periods of time. It is happening to me now, as my mother's long illness worsens into a fourth year of caregiving. As I ask for help and respite, both people she loves and people I love turn away from the situation. I receive platitudes and offers of prayer while family members head for the nearest exit or don't show up at all.

I don't know if there is such a thing as a "Sugar Jew" or a "Sugar Buddhist" or a "Sugar Moslem" or a "Sugar

Christian Scientist." Religion has nothing to do with being a "Sugar Christian," even though flowery phrases are often used by those suffering from this condition to put words as a screen in front of the situation.

I used to think it was a form of denial. It is. I used to think that it was a form of distancing. It is. I used to think that it was a form of fastidious distaste for the less-than-pleasant conditions of life. It is all that too. But what it really is, is fear—fear that you will be found wanting or that you won't be able to stand it or that you'll "catch death" if you're around it long enough; fear that you will melt into a puddle on the sidewalk if anyone rains on your parade.

Understanding the reasons behind this fear has helped me to conquer my own fear and has helped me to understand when people walk away when they are needed. (But I don't much like it.)

I believe that you learn responsibility, the ability to respond to others by practice. And sometimes it's difficult. And sometimes you think you can't do it anymore. And sometimes you're the one standing in the middle of the storm while everyone else is on an extended vacation. But you won't melt. You can't. Your grandmother won't hear of it.

"And when you feel like 'What can I do?' just know that your showing up and holding love in your mind means you are bringing the power of God. . . . If you will just show up, He will tell you what to do. . . . You will become transformed through an attitude of service. Just don't run away. The *only* enemy is your tendency to want to shut down and run away. The only thing to fear is the fear itself. Just stand forth and ask God continuously: 'Open my heart and we'll do everything right.' "

–MARIANNE WILLIAMSON *(Gifts for the Living)*

"Life is difficult. This is a great truth, one of the greatest truths. It is a great truth because once we see truly see this truth, we transcend it. Once we truly know that life is difficult—once we truly understand and accept it—then life is no longer difficult. Because once it is accepted, the fact that life is difficult no longer matters."

–M. SCOTT PECK *(The Road Less Traveled)*

Self-Discipline

DESTINY AND DISCIPLINE

I HAVE MET SOME VERY INTERESTING people recently. One is a woman who was first a battered wife with two small children to raise, then a middle-manager. Now she is a minister. Amazing but true.

I have another dear friend who is a renaissance woman. She can usually be found mastering eleven things by next Tuesday. She is currently studying to become a medical anthropologist, working as a tax accountant, apprenticing in midwifery, conducting search and rescue on the weekends, and oh yes, in her spare time she sings in a jazz cafe!

A man I know recently left his job working for the hospitals to run a bookstore with his lady-love in a small town in Colorado.

A woman, a practicing lawyer who used to work for the state, is now doing—of all things!—costuming for Shakespeare festivals.

But I also have a solid, down-to-earth friend who cannot understand how a turn of events could catapult a person into another field of work entirely. In two or three more years she will retire from the local school system. Then she will do what she wants—start her own business, travel, see the world. She wonders how a person zig-zags into more than one endeavor. She thinks, although she does not say it, that perhaps they are not disciplined. I have another friend who has gritted her teeth through countless years of working for a bureaucratic boss in a city services system. "Only six more years and then I can qualify for my pension." Her health problems escalate, while her energy level goes down. "I can stand it," she says. "It's just a matter of discipline."

I love all my friends. I would not presume to tell them—well, not more than once or twice anyway—what to do with their lives. I hate it myself, when I am advised, by people who have my best interests at heart, that I need to be more practical. "At least you're self-disciplined," they conclude. "You could do anything, because you're the most self-disciplined person I know."

No, I'm not. Yes, I'm self-disciplined, but mostly it's a matter of being in my destiny, instead of searching for it or waiting for it to appear on my doorstep. My brave friends try out new careers until they find their perfect fit. My cautious friends stay where they are, waiting for retirement. Either one or both is OK with me. I'm usually too busy to pay much attention, unless (God forbid) one of them asks my advice, in which case I'm off and running.

When I was raising four sons as a single parent, the

question of self-discipline didn't arise. Survival was my watchword then. I was a fierce lioness protecting and feeding my cubs. I was younger and had more stamina and energy, and vowed that nothing would stand in my way. And so I took a number of jobs that fed my family, knowing that these jobs were only a means to an end. Little did I know that even then, everything I learned would be used later on, as fodder for my writing career. Nothing was wasted. But it didn't look like a straight line upward. It looked like an up-and-down, peaks-and-valleys, highs-and-lows graph. If anyone had measured, I was all over the map. I was learning. I was growing. I was surviving. I was always a writer then too, even if the poems were stashed on top of the refrigerator, where sticky little hands could not scatter them. Even if self-discipline looked like nine to five, and then a later shift as well. But I knew.

What did I know? That someday both destiny and self-discipline would converge, and then everything I had learned would come together to be used. Instead of feeling like the old mule in harness with someone—myself!—cracking a whip over my head in self-discipline, now I can take the tools of self-discipline and use them to flow forward creatively. I am in my own true place. I am in my destiny.

Yours looks different. Maybe you're hopscotching all

over the place, trying on careers like you try on dresses, seeing what fits. Maybe you're a straight line, knowing that what you do is steady and cumulative and valuable just as it is. I don't know your path. I took one less traveled by. And got to where I am because somewhere along that path, self-discipline and destiny met each other.

*Are you in your destiny? If not, who or
what is keeping you from your true place in the world?*

•INTENTION•

I am willing to meld my destiny and my self-discipline so that I can express the essence of myself, so that I can experience my true place in the world. And so it is.

"Discipline doesn't have to be about restriction. It can be about freedom, it can be about openness, it can be about more rather than less."

–BATYA ZAMIR

"The seed of God is in us. Given an intelligent and hardworking farmer, it will thrive and grow up to God, whose seed it is; and accordingly its fruits will be God-nature. Pear seeds grow into pear trees, nut seeds into nut trees, and God Seed into God."

–MEISTER ECKHART

Self-Reliance

"STREET ENDS. NO OUTLET."

WHENEVER I FEEL SORRY FOR MYSELF, which is less and less as the years move on, I go outside before dawn, sit on the terrace, and watch the sun come up and the houses come to life. And I remember Cantey Street.

I see a very frightened, very determined young woman of thirty, a single parent with four sons to raise, no education, no money, no skills.

I had just moved back to Texas from Mexico City, where I had lived a far more glamorous life. Now I was starting over, in the mid-60s, with a job as an employee personnel trainer for a local department store and a second job in Dallas at the Apparel Mart on the weekends. That's when my mother and grandmother helped out with the children. During the week, I paid a dollar a day (each) for childcare. That was $20 a week. The house, I remember, cost $60 a month to rent, plus utilities and phone. I had a fifteen-year-old car and exactly $12 a week for groceries. The second job paid for incidentals, like clothes and shoes and school supplies and books.

And what did I do that first year I moved back? Each night, after the children were put to bed, I sat on the cement steps of the horrible, paint-peeling, roof-leaking, linoleum-cracking house on Cantey Street and I stared at what was in front of me. The house was in a cul-de-sac on a corner where the trains went by. They would switch tracks at ten o'clock each night. That's when I went to bed. I had to get up at five. That's when they switched tracks again. 5:00 A.M. There was a street sign right in front of me, under the street light, there where the trains switched over to their alternate routes. It said, "Street Ends. No Outlet." Night after night, I watched that sign. It was a signal of my despair. "Street Ends. No Outlet."

After watching that sign for a year, one night I got up from the porch steps and said aloud to myself, "No."

The next day I applied for school loans and scholarships. I went to college at night and worked at the department store in the daytime. Later, when I lost my job at the department store, I switched to days at college and a patchwork of adult education teaching jobs, plus my weekend job. Once I remember, I was juggling three jobs and going to college at the same time.

People tried to make me feel guilty. "You should stay home and take care of your kids." Yeah, right! On what? "You should find a good man and settle down." I had no time for anything except survival. "Won't your kids suffer if you're busy working and going to school all the time?" Maybe. But it beats starving. They, at least, will have a future. As would I. Because I had a plan. I would finish college, get my degree, continue with fellowships to graduate school, teach college, and then my children could go to college free. It was the only plan I knew that would take me out of Cantey Street and "Street Ends. No Outlet."

Oh yes. I had one additional goal. I would buy a house for me and my children. I would move away from Cantey Street. By a series of serendipitous circumstances, a year later I was able to do just that. I bought a house in fore-closure, pledging future teaching earnings. The house was on College Avenue, a sign, I thought, of better days to come. Since this is an essay and not a novel, I will not tell you the whole story of my life. Details aren't important. How many thousands of single mothers have been here before? I was not the first, nor the last. I understand that a few men, too, have raised themselves by their bootstraps. This isn't an essay about having. It's an essay about doing.

Self-reliance takes many forms. I've started over again and again in my life. Maybe you have too. Maybe there has been a pivotal moment where you said to yourself the one word "No." No, I will not continue this way. I will switch tracks. I will take an alternate route. I will not give in to despair. I am strong enough and brave enough to change my life.

There is a postscript to this story. I sit outside at dawn and watch the sun catch the name on the sign at the end of the street where I now live, one house over from the corner. The name on the sign is West Cantey Street. One hundred yards from my house. One block from the university. Three miles, more or less, as the crow flies, from that first house on Cantey Street, the one by the railroad tracks. I've moved across the country, I've traveled the world, I've lived a lifetime since that first house on Cantey Street.

Three miles and thirty years. It's a long, long way from Cantey Street. Maybe you've been there too. Do you honor how very far you've come? Do you honor your self-reliance, your determination, your perseverance, your sheer grit? Do you? I do. It's a long, long way from Cantey Street. I'll never go there again.

Dear God,

Thank You for Your guidance that has led me forward all these years. Thank You for teaching me self-reliance. Thank You for bringing me this far. Each day I will go forward trusting in You and trusting in myself, knowing that all things work together for good in my life. I am grateful for Your compass that has led me to my own true place. And so it is. *Amen.*

"I am sure that most of us, looking back, would admit that whatever we have achieved in character we have achieved through conflict; it has come to us through powers hidden deep within us, so deep that we didn't know we had them, called into action by the challenge of opposition and frustration, the weights of life keep us going."

–J. WALLACE HAMILTON

"Our roots resemble those of trees: Heavy winds and tempests make us stronger and dig our roots deeper into the soil. We must gain strength from every gust of adversity."

–ROBERT MULLER *(A Planet of Hope)*

Serenity

SPACE SERENE

MY HOME IS THE OUTER REFLECTION of my inner self. In it, I live and work and play and dream and create and love. Spacious and full of light, it is seventy-five years old, with an arched curved gothic doorway, weathered plain wood that says "welcome," and twenty-eight windows, most of them antique twelve-paned, to reflect the masses of green trees that surround it. Its floors are the original Texas pine, while its nooks and crannies astonish one unexpectedly, as does the mosaic tiled fireplace inlaid with original antique designs of birds. Everywhere you look, from peaceful high ceilings and walls done in dove gray with fresh white trim, from "twenties" mosaic tiles in bathrooms, to the sweep of the doorways, one room opening spaciously into the next, on and on for an infinity of doorways, all speak to me of a safe and beautiful place, a creative haven. My home is my space serene.

My home is surrounded by four churches and a university. Every hour on the hour, the carillon chimes music that soars to each nearby home. The bells chime again for every rite of passage—wedding, funeral, graduation—that occurs in this neighborhood.

When I reflect on all the places I have lived, all over the world, I am bemused at ending up here, in an old-fashioned neighborhood, in the town of my childhood.

The 125-year-old magnolia tree in my front yard was planted when my own forefathers and foremothers came across the prairies from Tennessee after the Civil War and stopped here, on a bluff overlooking a river, where there was a fort and not much else except their own hands and hearts and dreams. The tree speaks to me of continuity through generations.

And so I find, to my surprise, that I am rooted here. This is the ground of my being. This is where my heart is. Here is my space serene.

Is your dwelling place merely a place you live in or have you made it into your home? How can you make your living space more beautiful and blessed? Do you cherish your home as a reflection of your serenity? Do you extend comfort to yourself and to others through your home?

· INTENTION ·

I now choose to make my home into a beautiful and serene reflection of my life. As I evolve, so will my home, until everyone who comes into this space will feel welcome and joyful.

Bless this house, O Lord I pray.
Keep it safe from day to day.
May my home be wide and warm,
Free from hatred, free from harm.
May its strong and sheltering arms
Cherish those who seek its warmth
I share my haven, food, and rest.
May all who enter here be blessed.
Amen.

"Dwell as near as possible to the channel in which your life flows."

–HENRY DAVID THOREAU

Service

THE ARMS AND LEGS OF GOD

WHEN I VISIT MY MOTHER in the skilled nursing facility where she is spending the rest of her days, I am struck by the cheerfulness and respect that the staff shows to the elderly residents. There is an air of thoughtfulness and gentleness that permeates the walls and spills over into the lives of the people who are sequestered there.

I noticed one day that the physical therapists wore wide webbed belts, like harnesses, with all manner of clasps and hooks attached. They looked a little like skydivers, fastened about as they were with all manner of tool and harness. Yes, skydivers walking patiently with the temporarily earthbound elderly.

"I love my physical therapy," my mother exclaimed to me on a good day. "This is what they do. They hook you onto them and then you can walk with them safely and they teach you how to walk straight, and how to turn, and how to balance. You put your steps with theirs, or maybe they put their steps with yours, something like that. That way," she said, and there were tears in her eyes, even then, as she struggled to explain, "you don't fall. You are held safely to them."

My mother has fallen several times in the last four months. The main injury that placed her in this skilled nursing facility shattered three ribs and cut her head open, necessitating seventeen stitches above her eye. Subsequent falls reactivated old fractures suffered over the last three years of gradual deterioration with Parkinson's disease.

A meditation teacher who has been helpful to me told me once, "Your work is to be the arms and legs of God."

I think of the gentle, patient physical therapists, who hook my mother onto their webbed belts and match her steps, side by side. Their work consists of being the arms and legs of God.

A prayer that has sustained me over many years consists of just these few words. "Hands, head, and heart now work together in harmony for God and good."

Whether we are corporate giants or serving the homeless, whether we write books or teach children, whether we sweep streets or build monuments, we can do the work that is ours to do in a spirit of prayerful service. Then our work is indeed being the arms and legs of God, the hands and heart and head of God. And when we match our steps to others, creating a sense of safety, a sense of respect, then we are both blessed and blessing. Our work is sacred and we serve the world.

"May the blessing of light be on you, light without and light within. May the blessed sunshine shine on you and warm your heart till it glows like a great peat fire, so that the stranger may come and warm himself at it, and also a friend."

–OLD IRISH BLESSING

How are you the arms and legs of God?
How do you serve and bless others?

"The service we render for others is really the rent we pay for our room on this earth."

–WILFRED GRENFELL

I don't know what your destiny will be, but one thing I do know: the only ones among you who will be really happy are those who have sought and found how to serve."

–ALBERT SCHWEITZER

Simplicity

THE GREEN CATHEDRAL OF THE TREES

THERE IS A PLACE that I love, a place I go each morning, a place that waits for me. When I step outside the side door of my old-fashioned, cozy, comforting house that welcomed me from the first moment I saw it, I can turn my eyes to the left and see houses and neighbors and joggers and cars and all the paraphernalia of a busy city neighborhood. If I look ahead of me, I see walls of honeysuckle and wild roses, dividing my house from the one next door. If I look down, there are irises of every color, shape, and size along my path, and if I turn to the right, which I do slowly every morning, there is nothing to see but a yellow wooden garage with redwood trim and a sharply-pitched shingled roof (filled with stored books, of course!). Behind it, above it, and on each side of it, a canopy of pecan trees frame the yellow garage as if in a painting.

This is where I pray. Once I reached out and broke off a leaf of the pecan tree that stood closest to the cement walkway where I park my car. The leaf was warm and slightly dusty, juicy inside. It was not cement. It was alive.

In the famous poem, "The Force that through the

Green Fuse drives the Flower," the fierce and lyrical Welsh poet Dylan Thomas speaks of the force in creation that drives the plant and the tree and the flower, and that drives you and me as well.

I believe that this force is God: God within the warm and dusty leaf and the pecan that swells, bursts, and falls to the ground, God in the green cathedral of the trees that arches and protects the yellow garage with the redwood trim and the house with its arched gothic doorways and its brown shingled roof, the house with the honeysuckle and irises around it.

Sometimes I rest my back against the gray-ringed bark of the largest tree, the one whose branches arch and soar and rustle and protect, and with a cup of cinnamon tea laced with honey, I stand and rest and breathe and think. No, that is not quite true. I don't think. I don't plan. I don't implore, beseech, beg. I don't frame words to match thoughts to make sense. I just receive.

What do I receive? It varies, according to season and state of mind. When my mother was ill for over four years (and is still) I received comfort. The branches seemed to arch above me protectively, as if to hold me in their arms, or to hold her, should she decide to soar to heaven and leave her struggling, crumbling body behind.

When I have work deadlines that seem impossible to meet, I go and stand under that green cathedral of the trees, and I am silent, letting the churning processing of words subside, and I rest my eyes on the yellow garage as if I am in a museum and an important American representational painting has caught and held my eye. Its simplicity and solidity endures.

And what has any of this to do with soul making? Soul recognizing? Soul development? Everything. Nothing. You choose.

Once I thought that in order to find the secrets of the universe, it was necessary to travel to mountaintops, study indigenous peoples and cultures, roam uncharted seas. God in church and God in history and God in books. Once I thought that God was everywhere else. Everywhere but here.

Simplicity. The sacred in the ordinary. Find yours. Find your own green cathedral, your own yellow garage. Breathe in honeysuckle and wild roses, if you can. Or merely lean your weight against a sturdy, ancient tree. And receive.

May I give and receive simplicity in all that I think, say, feel, and do. May I find the sacred in the ordinary and share it with the world.

"People say that what we're all seeking is a meaning for life. I don't think that's what we're really seeking. I think that what we're really seeking is an experience of being alive, so that our life experiences on the purely physical plane will have resonances within our innermost being and reality, so that we can actually feel the rapture of being alive."

–JOSEPH CAMPBELL *(The Power of Myth)*

Solitude

GROWING THE SOUL IN SOLITUDE

WHY EVER WOULD YOU CONSIDER solitude as a virtue? As a soul quality to be developed and nurtured? I was asked that question recently by a new acquaintance who insisted that everything is relationship and that only as we are in relationship to one another are we growing spiritually. Specifically, she felt only if we are in a male-female intimate relationship are we growing spiritually.

I don't think so. I told her so, politely. I mentioned, briefly, other types of relationships that are tools for personal and spiritual growth. Like children dying or ill parents or deep friendships. Like a relationship with your work. Like a deep and trusted relationship with God. We skirted around each other politely, neither giving an inch.

I think that now, if I had the chance, I would tell her about my relationship with solitude. It is my dear and trusted friend. It is an integral, life-affirming, growth-enhancing part of my life. I would not part with it for all the world.

If I don't have enough time to myself and for myself, I become cranky and jittery, like a child who has stayed up past her bedtime and will break into tears at any moment.

My solitude is a hard-won gift I have given myself. Oh, the years when solitude was only possible if I got up an hour early and went to bed an hour later than anyone else in the family! Oh, the times of adjustment to working in offices or teaching school, or in sales, or running my own company, or traveling on business. Even now, no matter how enriching the trip, I always run thankfully home to my serene and spacious solitude.

I do love being with other people. Just not all the time. For all the times that I have told my friends that I am working, please, no phone calls or dropping in, there are a hundred more times that I drop whatever I am doing and welcome them with open arms. But afterwards, I have my solitude. I have my cherished, creative, enchanted solitude.

The self grows in relationship to other people. Yes, that's true. And the soul grows in private time, time spent apart, without hurry, worry, bustle, or talk. The soul grows in contemplation, reflection, meditation, prayer. The soul grows in being as well as doing. Then of course you take the soul lessons out into the doing part of your world. There is a time for action and interaction. But the precious times, for me, are my times of solitude. Where I am really not alone at all.

❦

Do you have a solitary ritual? A solitary pleasure?
How has solitude contributed to your Soulwork?

· INTENTION ·

I bless my solitude. I honor my solitude. I thank God for my solitude. I am creative in my solitude.

"All paths lead to the same goal: to convey to others what we are. And we must pass through solitude and difficulty, isolation and silence, in order to reach forth to the enchanted place where we can dance our clumsy dance and sing our sorrowful song—but in this dance or in this song there are fulfilled the most ancient rites of our conscience in the awareness of being human and of believing in a common destiny."

–PABLO NERUDA

"Our language has wisely sensed the two sides of being alone. It has created the word 'loneliness' to express the pain of being alone. And it has created the word 'solitude' to express the glory of being alone."

–PAUL TILLICH (*The Eternal Now*)

"When one is a stranger to oneself then one is estranged from others too. If one is out of touch with oneself, then one cannot touch others. How often in a large city, shaking hands with my friends, I have felt the wilderness stretching between us. Both of us were wandering in arid wastes, having lost the springs that nourished us—or having found them dry. Only when one is connected to one's own core is one connected to others, I am beginning to discover. And, for me, the core, the inner spring, can best be refound through solitude."

–ANNE MORROW LINDBERGH *(Gift from the Sea)*

Talent/Intentions/Abilities

USE WHAT YOU HAVE IN THE HOUSE

"At that point in life where your talents meet the needs of the world, that is where God wants you to be." For many years, long before I was published as a writer, I kept those words pasted on my old manual Smith-Corona typewriter. My talents or my abilities or my destiny seemed to be, for many years at least, making a living for my four children and myself, going to school, teaching school, and working at an endless variety of second jobs in order to make ends meet. Echoes of old tapes often played in my head. "Who do you think you are, to think that you are a writer? Who do you think you are, to think that you can be published? Who do you think you are, to think you can make a living as a writer?" I answered those tapes as best as I could, through all the discouragement and exhaustion and time constraints. "I am a writer." So the second and third parts of the equation, the publication and the livelihood, had to come at some point. Of course I was also a number of other labels, from mother to teacher. But my primary purpose, the essence of who I was, the who I was in my bones, was a writer. That single-mindedness carried me through.

My grandmother, who fed a household of ten women during the Second World War, often said when times got tough, "We will use what we have in the house." I used what I had. I continued. And by using every insight, every situation, every competency, I grew into a place where my talents met the needs of the world.

How presumptuous! you might say, to think that God is watching over you, using your talents. How presumptuous to even think that you have talents that God may have need of. I heard those echoes too.

But surely we are here for a purpose. And surely we each have a unique and valuable and needed destiny, a place where our intentions and our abilities can flourish, bear fruit, be used.

Once I wrote a poem that began, "Let my words be a candle to the Lord." I was not particularly religious at the time, but the poem spilled out with words like soaring and pouring yourself out to be heard. It was a poem of ecstasy. I don't know where it came from. Later a friend of mine, who was a singer and a songwriter, took my words and put music to them. She did this in a kindly but embarrassed way, because she was used to writing pop rock and she did not share the emotion of the lyrics. Recently I took several hours to look for both the poem and the tape of the song, wondering if the emotion still existed within the words that were a gift from me to God.

I could not find the song or the lyrics in their entirety, but on the practice tape, my friend's voice soared with such joy and beauty that it brought tears to my eyes. The words reaffirmed me and sustained me: "Let my words be a candle to the Lord."

I was talking to a man about intention and destiny recently. "I have the abilities, I have the intention, I have the discipline and the energy. So," I asked him (because everyone is my teacher), "how do I make a quantum leap forward in the quality and quantity of the books I write? How can they be better? How can I be excellent instead of merely adequate?" What I was really asking was, "How can my words be heard?"

He suggested that I sit in meditation each morning and ask those same questions. "But I already meditate every morning," I told him. "And I often ask questions and I often listen until I receive clear answers."

"But do you ask those specific questions?"

"Well, no," I said. "It seems kind of conceited, kind of self-elevating, kind of, well—presumptuous." There's that word again!

"How can your destiny enfold you," he then asked me, "if you are judging it before it comes to you? How can you be in your destiny if you do not allow your destiny to come into you?" Wow!

Of course I took his advice. How could I not? I had

signposts along the way. I had a quotation pasted on an old typewriter and now facing me as I work on my computer. I had my grandmother's words, echoing down the corridors of time. "Use what you have in the house." I had a poem and a song and a twelve-year-old practice tape to remind me of words I once flung into the sky with joy and reverence.

How could I not be in my destiny? How could I not use the abilities given to me by God? Impossible.

Surely you have some of the same doubts that I have had? Surely you have wondered at your own temerity in asking for excellence in your chosen path?

"At that point in life where your talents meet the needs of the world, that is where God wants you to be." And that is where you must be. Sooner or later, your abilities and your intentions, bolstered by practice and prayer, will bring your destiny to you. You will feel it in your bones. You will celebrate it in your words. You will be your destiny.

• I N T E N T I O N •

I am in my destiny. I am in my talents. I will use what I have in the house to go forward with my dreams. And so it is.

"Argue for your limitations and sure enough, they're yours."

–RICHARD BACH

"This is the true joy of life, the being used up for a purpose recognized by yourself as a mighty one; being a force of nature instead of a feverish, selfish little clod of ailments and grievances, complaining that the world will not devote itself to making you happy. I am of the opinion that my life belongs to the community, and as long as I live, it is my privilege to do for it whatever I can. I want to be thoroughly used up when I die, for the harder I work, the more I live. Life is no 'brief candle' to me. It is a sort of splendid torch which I have got hold of for a moment, and I want to make it burn as brightly as possible before handing it on to future generations."

–GEORGE BERNARD SHAW

Tenderness

TENDER-HEARTED WARRIORS

I HAVE A FRIEND who does something amazing every week. She gets up in a pulpit, in front of hundreds of parishioners, and presents the original prayer that she has written for the week. And the prayer falls into the hearts of the people who hear it.

She doesn't pull any punches with her prayers. She prays about Bosnia and the Oklahoma City bombing. She prays about hailstorms and the homeless.

I asked her how she did it. She told me of her own prayers for clarity and purpose, the same type of prayer I use whenever I sit down to write. But then she told me more. She told me about aikido.

"In aikido you do not try to overcome your opponent with force or fear. Instead you blend with the energy of your opponent. You become what I call a tender-hearted warrior. You use the energy not to conquer but to disarm. You prevail out of clarity and purpose and intention." (Ah, favorite words!)

I would like to be a tender-hearted warrior—to speak out against the great and the small injustices in the world, and with intent, set about to change, in even the smallest way, the balance in this world between war and peace, between love and fear. I believe this is done by healing the warring parts of myself that seek to dominate and control, and loving those parts of me as they struggle to change and learn. I believe that I can be a tender-hearted warrior to myself. Yet "faith without works is dead." So I believe, also, that I can then carry the tender-hearted warrior of myself out into the mundane world. Just like my friend.

Can you do the same? Whether you work to clean up your neighborhood or clean up your planet, whether you volunteer at a Thanksgiving soup kitchen or plan to feed the world, whether you run for politics or compose prayers, you too, are a part of the clarity and purpose and intention of the tender-hearted warrior. I pray that I may be also.

O God,

Teach us how to be tender-hearted warriors. Not mushy sentimentalists but instead to love wisely and with strength of focus. Teach us the courage of a warrior to stay on the path, yet infill us with a compassionate heart to stand up for justice, both for others and for ourselves when needed.

Thank You, God, for people who are tender-hearted warriors, who are courageous and compassionate, strong and vulnerable. May we be also. We ask in Your name, *Amen.*

–PRAYER BY THE REVEREND SANDRA LYDICK

Are you a tender-hearted warrior? Look back on your life experiences and review times in which you were both courageous and compassionate. How can you carry the qualities of a tender-hearted warrior into a current situation? Can you honor the people around you who exemplify the traits of a tender-hearted warrior? How can you learn from them?

• I N T E N T I O N •

I vow to act as a tender-hearted warrior in all that I think, feel, say, and do this week. I am becoming more courageous and compassionate every day. And so it is.

"Tenderness contains an element of sadness. It is not the sadness of feeling sorry for yourself or feeling deprived but it is a natural situation of fullness. You feel so full and rich, as if you were about to shed tears. Your eyes are full of tears, and the moment you blink, the tears will spill out of your eyes and roll down your cheeks. In order to be a good warrior, one has to feel this sad and tender heart. If a person does not feel alone and sad, he cannot be a warrior at all."

— CHOGYAM TRUNGPA *(Shambhala: The Sacred Path of the Warrior)*

"It is better to live one day as a lion than a hundred years as a sheep."

— ITALIAN PROVERB

"If a bird is flying for pleasure it flies with the wind, but if it meets danger it turns and faces the wind, in order that it may rise higher."

— CORRIE TEN BOOM

Tolerance

NO BORDERS

WHEN ASTRONAUT RUSSELL SCHWEICKART went to the moon, his life was changed through perspective and distance. He reported in awe: "The contrast between that bright blue and white Christmas-tree ornament and the black sky, that infinite universe, and the size and significance of it really comes through. It is so small and so fragile, such a precious little spot in that universe, that you can block it out with your thumb. You realize that everything that means anything to you—all of history and art and death and birth and love, tears and joys, all of it, is on that little blue and white spot out there which you can cover with your thumb. And you realize from that perspective that you have changed, that there is something new, that the relationship is no longer what it was."

Wouldn't it be wonderful if we could see and know, as did Russell Schweickart, the planet Earth in its wholeness, its oneness, its meaning, and have that seeing change us? Wouldn't it be wonderful if world leaders could realize what he has realized? There are no borders. From space, there are no borders. Differences, yes. Tribes, yes. Weapons, most assuredly. But as we move closer to the next millennium, there is a groundswell of opinion every-where that we either learn to live in peace or all blow up together.

I've thought a lot about tolerance. I've thought about the times, years ago, when my mother, who always wanted to be a teacher, began to work in the schools as a teacher's aide. They assigned her to a multiracial elemen-tary school in a tough neighborhood. My mother was astonished that the children at first didn't seem to like her. She was called names. One boy kicked her. Another spat at her. Eventually her inherent loving kindness and genuine desire to reach the children paid off. But it was the first time in her sheltered life that my mother had experienced prejudice in reverse. I give her a lot of credit. She overcame her own learned bias against people of color by choosing to work directly with the children. She also set limits. She would not be treated badly because she was of a different background and color. The chil-dren and staff grew to love and respect her.

When I worked in the AIDS crisis in Los Angeles and San Francisco, I met people who had been a long time in the war. They were shell-shocked, the caregiving wound-ed. One or two were outraged that I, who had in fact been there since the early days of AIDS, would be a part of their fight, would take up their banner. "We are the ones who have suffered," they told me. "How dare you trespass on our territory? How can you, a middle-aged, straight woman, understand our pain?"

I could, and I did. Dissolved my own ignorance, raised my consciousness. I labored in the fields of death, dying, and despair. And no one has challenged my right to be there since.

Aren't we all aiming for the same result? To treat one another respectfully and tolerantly, whether our differences are of color, of gender, of lifestyle. To see the individuality within each person, no matter how different they may appear to us on the outside. To see the essence of each person. To honor both their differences and their dignity.

How else can we work together for the common good? How else can we love our neighbor? And if we are not yet prepared to love our neighbor, can we at least tolerate our differences? Can we, at least, be kind?

I remember the time I first saw these words in Robert Muller's *A Planet of Hope:* "Arnold Toynbee once was asked what he would recommend as the single most important means for achieving a better world. He answered: 'If only people could be kinder to each other.'"

To refuse to engage in hate is the first step. Martin Luther King, Jr., said it so eloquently, "I have decided to stick with love. Hate is too great a burden to bear."

So have I. How else can I live together with you and

you and you on one planet that, from a God's-eye view, has no borders?

I choose to be more tolerant. I choose to walk in peace with others, knowing there are no borders, there is only good in each of us. And so it is.

When Apollo XV went to the moon, another astronaut, James B. Irwin, carried a prayer written by James Dillet Freeman, poet laureate of Unity. The prayer, entitled "I Am There," was left on the moon for future space voyagers. Here is a small portion of that prayer.

> "I am in all.
> Though you may not see the good, good is there,
>   for I am there.
> I am there because I have to be, because I am.
> Only in Me does the world have meaning; only out of
> Me does the world take form; only because of Me
>   does the world go forward.
> I am the law on which the movement of the stars and
>   the growth of living cells are founded.
> I am the love that is the law's fulfilling . . .
> . . . Beloved, I am there."

"I believe that every man and woman represents humanity. We are all different as to intelligence, health, talent. Yet we are all one. We are all saints and sinners, adults and children, and no one is anyone's superior or judge. We have all been awakened with the Buddha, crucified with Christ, and we have all killed and robbed with Genghis Khan, Stalin, and Hitler."

–ERICH FROMM

Trust

MONEY, TRUST, AND SHOVELS

I DON'T WORRY ABOUT MONEY ANYMORE. I used to. Born in the Great Depression, nourished on tales of "not enough," I spent almost sixty years striving, struggling, measuring, begging, pleading, cajoling. Surviving. Whether I was raising four children alone, putting myself through college and graduate school, teaching school, running my own business, writing books. Supporting myself. Supporting others. I was an expert on frugality, making do, doing without. I was a thrifty recycler long before the '90s. Now I am a not-so-young, single, female freelancer. Government statistics do not bode well for me. But. Yet. I don't worry about money anymore. I have enough.

In her marvelous book *Money Freedom,* Patricia Remele teaches how we can see money as a servant, a tool for the good we wish to accomplish in the world. Her book is about trust and abundance and all those other good affirmative processes I have been working with for a number of years. But now, somehow, I "get" it.

I remember especially the story about shovels. Money has such connotations in our Western society, so many emotions, especially deep-seated fears, attached to it and to the pursuit of it, that it's a wonder any of us manage to pay our bills, support our families, and follow our dreams. The author suggests that we begin to break the hold that centuries of money sayings have had on us by substituting the word "shovels" in every conversation we have with ourselves about money. Try "The love of shovels is the root of all evil" or "Time is shovels" and begin to break the associations of fear and desperation about lack and scarcity.

I began experiencing a wealth of ideas when I applied the exercises in this book. I took a long look at many other books that had assisted me on my journey of abundance, books that I had used over the years with varying success at the time. I realized that it all came down to the idea of trust. Trust that I would be provided for. Trust that what I did mattered. Trust in my own value. Trust in God, of course, but not as someone on high who would fulfill my laundry list of wishes, but as someone I could trust to steer me on my journey.

I took a quantum leap forward in trust. I began by trusting myself more. That inner trust led to inner creativity. This translated into a sense of well-being and abundance in several areas of my life.

I have written before about a sense of spiritual movement—that process of transformation or renewal that leads us to know that where once we learned from pain and only from pain, now, even through the dark times of our lives, we can learn from joy. This trusting process happens gradually, as we affirm and question and listen to the answers we receive. This process continues over a lifetime. It continues even through the pain, struggle, and unresolved areas of sorrow in our lives. It continues even in such mundane areas as money.

I trust myself more. I trust others more. I trust the universe more. I trust God more. I trust that there will always be enough for me.

And I have more than enough shovels to continue.

•INTENTION•

I choose to practice trust in all that I think, feel, say, and do. I apply this trust to money and all other forms of abundance in my daily life. There is plenty to share and plenty to spare. And so it is.

Dear God,
Your wealth is in my heart, O God. Trusting, trusting, trusting, trusting, God, I am trusting You now. And so it is. *Amen.*

"An authentically empowered human being . . . is a human being that does not release its energy except in love and trust. "

–GARY ZUKAV *(Thoughts from the Seat of the Soul)*

"He that knows that enough is enough will always have enough."

–LAO-TZU *(Tao Te Ching)*

Will

WILL, FREE WILL, AND GOD'S WILL

ONE OF MY FRIENDS, whom I've mentioned before, is famous for her good sense and practical advice. She is far more patient than I am and listens to her friends' concerns for hours at a time. She revels in being a helper. She's got it down pat.

One day she and a couple of other women were sitting around the kitchen table talking about the same old problems. One friend of hers, who has always had difficulty making up her mind in situations and has had even more difficulty in following through on any action, was bemoaning the fact that God never listened to her. (God didn't have to. My friend is the best listener in town.) "I just want to do the Lord's will," she kept saying. "Why won't the Lord help me? I just want to do his will." My no-nonsense friend exclaimed, "Quit waiting on God's will. God is not going to do your work for you. Get yourself going and do it yourself."

How often have we waited for things to change, hoping and praying that if we were good enough and asked enough and were patient enough and—God forbid!—immobile enough, we would know God's will and then we would do it. Or better yet, it would be done for us.

I believe that a strong and able will, including will-power, means that we are to go forward as best we can on our own steam, trusting in Divine Providence and spiritual guidance and a little nudge or so along the way.

I used to get my will and "Thy will be done" confused. I still do sometimes. We talked about this in Week Two when we explored acceptance and surrender, followed by action.

A strong will can carry you forward into spiritual adventures and satisfying work. A trusting will can harmonize relationships and lead you through the storm. So that's good. But that's only part of the equation.

I pray often for "the highest good of all concerned" in any situation I am facing. I pray for "this or something better," since I don't always know what is best for me in the long run. I pray "Thy will be done" when I release long-standing concerns to the personal and provident and loving God in whom I believe.

And then I act on the guidance I have received. With all my will and all my power I go forward, trusting in the outcome.

God works through us, not for us, even in the use of will. So go forward on your own steam, on your own power, knowing that your will and God's will are united in good, that your will and God's will, together, will create the best outcome. And, if in doubt, pray "Thy will be done." Pray it a hundred times a day, if need be. Until your will and God's will are one.

Dear God,
Thy will be done. *Amen.*

"We all talk about free will and God's will without realizing that they are one and the same. Our free will is our free use of God's will, which is concentrated in our divine consciousness. This means that our intuitive guidance, our true aspirations, and our loving intentions all represent the will of our master Self—and to accept anything less than the highest and greatest in life is to deny the will."

–JOHN RANDOLPH PRICE *(The Angels within Us)*

Wisdom/Understanding

WISDOM WOMEN

I LEARN FROM EVERYONE I meet. So it is not surprising that when a group of friends gather for our women's spiritual group, that wisdom and understanding tiptoe in with the nourishing grace of being with like-minded people about whom I care deeply.

Last week we started our group by helping a young woman become clear about the difference between the "clatter in my head versus the rock inside me." Her words. By the end of the discussion, she had identified the rock "that guides me"—which she had once thought of as immovable and opposed to her outer wishes, opinions, and judgments—as the strength of her core self. This rock led her by instinct to make the right choices for her life. "Oh, like wisdom," she exclaimed, and that led inevitably to a wide-ranging, free-wheeling discussion of just what wisdom looked like in each of our lives.

For one woman, wisdom was sorting out and discarding everything that she wasn't at this time in her life and discovering for herself everything that she was. She had started doing this with her business, and the process of sorting had continued into every area of her life.

For another woman, wisdom was moving from basic Metaphysics 101 in which she once denied everything but the positive in her life. Now, she explained eloquently, wisdom consisted of embracing the dark as well as the light, the tragedies as well as the triumphs, and living life passionately and full-out, no matter what the circumstances, without running away, without avoidance.

For another woman, her belief system had come full circle, from years of feeling inadequate and not enough just as she was, to a powerful expression of love at the central core of her being, and then expressing that love through her work and friendships, until her life was one of embracing the love all around her.

There were other differing belief systems, from a deepening resurgence of faith, to a no-nonsense attitude about commonsense living.

All of these women were right, for wisdom does not come all at once from on high, although you can certainly ask for wisdom and or understanding in your prayers and meditations. You can certainly ask to be guided through each new day and each new experience. You can ask and you can listen. All of these women, in their individual ways, did ask, did listen. They took this wisdom and understanding into themselves and then worked to refine and to live the truths that resonated within them, the truths that were true for them.

The truths that were true for them. Ah, now we're getting into paradox and confusion! And before we debate just how many angels can dance on the head of a pin or what truth, wisdom, or understanding is, let's take a moment to feel the nourishing wisdom that can come from many sources, many viewpoints, many faiths.

Enlightened wisdom, enlightened understanding, just like love, cannot be achieved until and unless one is willing to be comfortable with paradox and confusion.

Each woman in the room had her version of wisdom to guide her. Each woman was right. For it is in communing with our core self that we can stumble upon wisdom. It is in a resurgence of deep and abiding faith that we can find our own wisdom. It is in using the common-sense verities of generations that we can discover what works for us in the way of wisdom. It is in sorting out and discarding and then accepting that we can find wisdom. It is in embracing the love that we are and extending it to the world that we can find wisdom. It is in living full-out, passionately and creatively, and in asking for strength and courage and guidance and understanding in both the dark times and the light that we can experience wisdom.

And it is in coming together in a circle that we can illuminate our own private interior search, bring it forth, give it forth, share it with others, multiply it, refine it, resonate with it, revel in it.

Be the wisdom. Live the wisdom that you are. Nourish yourself with wisdom. Embrace wisdom in all your current understanding. And then share it with your friends.

❧

Dear Lord,
Help me to live in wisdom. Help me to be the wisdom I need, today and every day. Thank You. And so it is. *Amen.*

"Enlightened space, the place of unconditional love, cannot be achieved until and unless one is willing to be comfortable with paradox and confusion."

–RALPH WALKER

"All truly wise thoughts have been thought already thousands of times; but to make them truly ours, we must think them over again honestly, till they take root in our personal experience."

–JOHANN WOLFGANG VON GOETHE

Wonder

CLIMBING THE WINDMILL

LET ME TELL YOU one of my favorite things to do. It is to walk down wide and empty streets, just after dawn, and to welcome whatever comes to me.

There is an interesting and beautiful labyrinth of streets that go around and around in a curving maze of beauty. Along the streets are old-fashioned, imposing houses set back on a bluff overlooking the city proper, set above acres of parkland and zoo and wild woodland, set like a mysterious contrast between civilization and nature. These "Courts," as they are called, are a block and a half from my own house. I walk there often. And each time I walk, the past comes rushing up to meet me, to be remembered in joy or in fear. To be remembered, resolved, and reconciled.

There is a time of year that I often quail before. It is the time between July 4th and July 18th, a space of two weeks. Many of the significant events of my life—marriage, divorce, moves across the country, back and forth and back again, the loss of my business, the dying of specific dreams, and the death of my beloved son—took place in this corridor of time. I always wonder what will happen within the time-span of these days.

I walked my path around the curving courts one week-end morning as usual. The dogs were out at one house, so I crossed to the middle of the street and started walking down the open, empty road. At seven in the morning, the day was already so hot that my clothes stuck to me and my glasses slipped down over my nose, so perhaps it was true that for a moment I couldn't see clearly. But then I did. I looked around and such a sense of joy seized me that it almost threw me backward onto the macadam. There was no one out but me. I was the only woman in the world, walking down an empty street, just after dawn, with wildland on one side and civilization on the other.

My vague distress, with which I had started the walk, dissipated. My orderly, reasoning mind, looking for clues as to what was to come, fell away. I ceased ruminating on the past and fearing the future.

I took a deep breath and looked up at the almost cloudless sky. Blue and blue and more blue, a blue so vivid and clear it might have been painted. There was one huge white cloud that came purposefully toward me. I peered at it. And felt the force of something, a lurch of memory that threw me back in time to a day when I was six years old—the day I climbed the windmill and lived to tell the tale. In fact, I wrote a poem about the event years later. The memory is still so fresh and vivid that I could quote you every line even now.

We lived in a small town in New Mexico one summer and rented a place out in the country. It was the first time I had ever seen a windmill. I was an intrepid child. I wanted to get closer to the sky. So one day I climbed the windmill. I can still remember how it felt, the wind buffeting me, almost knocking me off each rung, and me steadily advancing. And when I got to the seat of the windmill, I remember that I could see valleys joined with hills and waters and skies into an entranced order I had never seen before. I was—literally—on top of the world.

My parents were frantic. They stood far below, yelling at me to get down, screaming at me at the same time to hold on. My father finally climbed the windmill and carried me down in his arms. But I was never scared. Why was it that back then, when I was a child, I was never frightened? How different it is today.

Here is the heart of the poem:

She was solid in space while the world whirled on
    without pause.
No terror involved. Even though
She didn't know much about windmills' laws,
There was the stretching of arms out to embrace
All of the clean clear thereness of space,
And she knew at least for a moment where she was.

Back to present time.

I don't know how long I stood there, rooted to the road, looking upward into the blue, tears rolling down my face. Then something shifted. Something changed. The day rearranged itself into accustomed patterns. I was walking the labyrinth of streets, instead of perched on the windmill with a God's-eye view and a child's-eye faith.

I pondered all this in my heart.

Maybe, I thought, when I could think again, it was a sign—to tell me that I can trust these days as well as any others. Maybe, I thought, it is time to accept memories as harbingers of peace and joy, rather than as bearers of fear and pain. Maybe, I thought, it was a gift from the past, with no meaning attached other than to receive.

I walked back home. Nothing bad happened to me. No disaster awaited me. No heroic measures were required of me. I walked back home in wonder, safe and joyous under the endless sheltering blue.

Dear God,
Here is my pledge. I will look in wonder, as a child again. I will dismiss all thoughts of a fearful future and exist in the joy of the morning. Thank You, God, that this is now so. *Amen.*

"If you have never heard the mountains sighing, or seen the trees of the field clapping their hands, do not think because of that they don't. Ask God to open your ears so you may hear it, and your eyes so you may see it, because, though few men ever know it, they do, my friend, they do."

–McCANDISH PHILIPS

"The soul should always stand ajar, ready to welcome the ecstatic experience."

–EMILY DICKINSON

"Let mystery have its place in you; do not be always turning up your whole ploughshare of self-examination, but leave a little fallow corner in your heart ready for any seed the wind may bring, and reserve a nook of shadow for the passing bird, keep a place in your heart for the unexpected guest, an altar for the unknown God."

–HENRI FREDERIC AMIEL

Conclusion

THE SOUL AND THE LEVELS OF LIGHT

WHEN I FIRST BEGAN THIS BOOK, I was full of trepidation. I knew that the process would be good for my character, good for my spiritual development, good for my soul. What I could not fathom was how it could be written. I had the idea that I would have to force pious thoughts into little boxes, that creativity and clarity and the yearning to experience, express, and expand (all qualities of the soul) would never fit within the strict confines of a year of spiritual work. But just as I learned about pulling clouds through a thermometer in order to bring chaos into form, so did I learn, through the daily concentration upon these fifty positive soul qualities, that I could change the form of my spiritual experience as well. I could remember and reflect and relearn. I could find the holy in the daily. I could look at life, mine, yours, ours, everyone's as an exquisite procession of insights. I could trust my seasons of the soul.

How personal it is for each of us. Books can give us metaphors for living, but we have to do our own living. We have to find our own way. Through the deep and through the dark. Through the high and through the holy. Through the everyday lessons and through the labyrinth. This book is one way.

I've often read that the process of spiritual development is very like that of peeling an onion. That is, layers and layers of the outside being loosened, peeled, discarded, so that the aromatic core, the heart of the onion, can be revealed. Maybe.

Recently the image that has come to me has nothing at all to do with onions. Nothing at all to do with the outside. Not of anyone and most certainly not of their soul. The image that comes to me is of densely packed, multidimensional, multilayered levels of light. And these levels of light are not only all around the person, they are the person. They emit from the core self within the person. They are the levels of light that comprise the soul. The soul is the interior light, the core. The levels of light are the levels of the soul expressed in form.

Now how does all this work? Bear with me. I believe that as we take these images of our inner light and then pray and meditate and ask and listen and give and receive and become aware of these levels of light, and especially of that core light, that tiny, flickering candle, that essence, that divine spark, that then the soul can begin to gently dislodge and dissolve all the levels of denser light that stand between the inner core and the outer world. As these levels of light are dissolved, the light of the soul can gently and wisely come forth. Each level of light, from the densest, next to the outer world, to the most hidden and most transparent, can gradually come to the fore. To be expressed in form.

If this is true (and it feels true to me), if we are indeed circles of light, encased in levels of light, then as we re-lease the levels, the levels of light go out into the world and touch the people around us in both mundane and magnificent ways.

There are no measurements for such a work as this. No boxes, no containers. There are only good people, shining, shining, shining, doing the work of the soul, level by level, layer by layer, light by light. Good by good.

❧

•INTENTION•

In my meditations and prayers, I will recognize and access the levels of light within me, more and more, day by day, so that the light of my being can reach out to oth-ers, so that the light of my being can touch the people around me, as their lights touch mine, in shared light, in shared goodness.

The Light of God surrounds you.
The Love of God enfolds you.
The Power of God protects you.
The Presence of God watches over you.
Wherever you are, God is.

–UNITY PRAYER FOR PROTECTION

"People are like stained-glass windows. They sparkle and shine when the sun is out, but when the darkness sets in, their true beauty is revealed only if there is a light from within."

–ELISABETH KUBLER-ROSS

"You are merely the lens in the beam. You can only receive, give, and possess the light as the lens does. If you seek yourself, "your rights," you prevent the oil and air from meeting in the flame, you rob the lens of its transparency. . . . You will know life and be acknowledged by it according to your degree of transparency, your capacity, that is, to vanish as an end, and remain purely as a means."

–DAG HAMMARSKJÖLD *(Markings)*

About the Author

BettyClare Moffatt, M.A., is a prominent writer and public speaker in the fields of AIDS, death and dying, grief recovery, and women's spirituality. She is the author of *Opening to Miracles: True Stories of Blessings and Renewal; Soulwork: Clearing the Mind, Opening the Heart, Replenishing the Spirit; When Someone You Love Has AIDS: A Book of Hope for Family and Friends; Journey Toward Forgiveness: Finding Your Way Home; Gifts for the Living: Conversations with Caregivers on Death and Dying;* and several other books.

Wildcat Canyon Press publishes books with a focus on spirituality, personal growth, women's issues, home, and family. Whether books of meditations, short essays, or how-to texts, they are designed to enlighten the hearts and souls of readers. For a catalog of our publications please write:

WILDCAT CANYON PRESS
2716 Ninth Street
Berkeley, CA 94710
Phone (510) 848-3600
Fax   (510) 848-1326